Big-Time Women from Way Back When

Jehanne of the Witches
by Sally Clark

&

A Woman's Comedy
by Beth Herst

Playwrights Canada Press
Toronto

Jehanne of the Witches © Copyright 1987 Sally Clark
A Woman's Comedy © Copyright 1991 Beth Herst

Playwrights Canada Press is the publishing imprint of the Playwrights Union of Canada: 54 Wolseley St., 2nd fl., Toronto, Ontario CANADA M5T 1A5
Tel: (416) 947-0201 Fax: (416) 947-0159

CAUTION: These plays are fully protected under the copyright laws of Canada and all other countries of The Copyright Union, and are subject to royalty. Changes to the scripts are expressly forbidden without the prior written permission of the authors. Rights to produce, film, or record, in whole or in part, in any medium or any language, by any group, *amateur or professional*, are retained by the authors. Those interested are requested to apply for all production rights for *A Woman's Comedy* to: Playwrights Union of Canada (PUC), and for *Jehanne of the Witches* - amateur rights contact PUC and professional rights contact:
Christopher Banks & Associates - 219 Dufferin St., Suite 305, Toronto, ON M6K 1Y9 (416) 530-4002.

No part of this book, covered by the copyright hereon, may be reproduced or used in any form or by any means - graphic, electronic or mechanical - without the prior written permission of the *publisher* execpt for excerpts in a review. Any request for photocopying, recording, taping or information storage and retrieval systems of any part of this book shall be directed in writing to The Canadian Reprography Collective, 214 King Street West, Suite 312, Toronto, Ontario, CANADA M5H 3S6

Playwrights Canada Press operates with the generous assistance of The Canada Council - Writing and Publishing Section, and Theatre Section, and the Ontario Arts Council.

Edited by Tony Hamill.

Canadian Cataloguing in Publication Data
Clark, Sally, 1953 -
    Big time women from way back when
Contents: Jehanne of the witches/Sally Clark --
    A woman's comedy/Beth Herst.
Plays
ISBN 0-88754-493-2
I. Herst, Beth. II. Title. III. Title: Jehanne of the witches.
IV. Title: A woman's comedy.
PS8555.L37B5 1993   C812'.54   C93-094734-7
PR9199.3.F67M6 1993

First edition: November, 1993
Printed and bound in Winnipeg, Manitoba, Canada.

Contents

Jehanne of the Witches 7

A Woman's Comedy 143

Jehanne of the Witches

by Sally Clark

Sally Clark was born in Vancouver. She moved to Toronto in 1973 and has been Playwright-in-Residence at Theatre Passe Muraille, The Shaw Festival Theatre, Buddies in Bad Times Theatre, and Nightwood Theatre. She spent a year at the Canadian Centre for Advanced Film Studies, where she directed the film based on her play *Ten Ways to Abuse an Old Woman*. Her plays include *Lost Souls and Missing Persons, Life Without Instruction, The Trial of Judith K.* (Playwrights Canada Press), and *Moo* (Playwrights Canada Press - Winner, Chalmers Best Canadian Play Award).

To my mother, Joan

Preface by Clarke Rogers

In a way, Sally Clark's *Jehanne of the Witches* is misnamed. The play, both in story and central thematic dilemma, is as much about Gilles de Rais as it is about Jehanne — Jeanne d'Arc, or, as she is also known, Joan of Arc. Indeed, approaching this play as another retelling of the Jeanne d'Arc story misses both the duality at its core and the drama of its theatrical narrative.

Although, as with all her work, Sally Clark has taken a distinctly feminine, if not absolutely feminist, point of view in her examination of Jeanne d'Arc — beginning with returning her given, pre-mythologized name. She has chosen to make a man, Gilles de Rais, her central character and protagonist. With deliberate irony, if not perversity, Clarke has chosen to view a female saint through the life of a male monster, a devil, the historical Bluebeard, seducer and murderer of hundreds of children.

This is the first of two radical approaches that Clark takes toward a drama which has attracted the interest of some of this century's major male playwrights. the second is that she refuses to see the character of Jehanne as either a victim of history or an idealistic popular heroine. The character she does offer is a far darker, far more threatening image of Joan than was conceived by any of the male heavyweights.

The theatricality of *Jehanne of the Witches* is woven into the very fabric of the piece. A play-within-a-play is being staged by one of the celebrated founders of French theatre — Gilles de Rais. His play, a true re-creation of the life of Jeanne d'Arc is historically true and made doubly accurate by the fact of his having been Jehanne's closet comrade-in-arms.

The fact that great barons, such as Gilles de Rais, served as generals and commanded armies is clearly recognized historically as a part of the nation-building process of the period, whether in France or England or elsewhere. However, the equally strong role these barons often took in the creation, collection, and encouragement of art appears less clearly acknowledged. As the sweet wind of the Renaissance blew north from Italy, it was often the great barons who welcomed the new ideas and gave them the opportunity to thrive. Theatre, and later music, required the resources only the Church or a noble could provide in order to exist at all, and it is worthwhile to note that Gilles de Rais was not alone as a noble playwright/producer. Many of the early English plays were written and performed by the great dukes and earls of the period. It could be argued that these plays were as effective in creating the idea of the modern national culture as were the armies these lords commanded.

Historically, Gilles de Rais' productions rivalled Hollywood in scale and ostentation, but Clark has focussed on a central, theatrical duality which reveals her deeper theme. In accordance with theatrical conventions of the time, Jehanne is played by a boy in Gilles' production. This boy actor, François, the butt of all Gilles' jibes (to put it delicately), is the polar opposite of the warrior saint — corrupt, weedy, whiny, and stupid. Since François is simultaneously playing Jehanne in Gilles' play and being played by a woman in Clark's play, the central dramatic issue of the story — the relationship of personal vision to historical processes — is able to be acted out in all its aspects within the relationship between he/she and Gilles. In fact, it becomes clear through the play that Clark's intention is to reveal that the saint and the monster are two parts of a larger, more primal whole, and that neither is what they appear to be. As I've mentioned, Jehanne, as presented here, is neither saint nor victim — rather she is one of a long line of female divines that society calls witches. As an initiate, she is able to blur her pagan Voices into the prevailing Catholicism, much as the rituals of the Old Religion were sanctified by Christian equivalents, but as the demands of the state increase, so does her inability to control the nature and direction of the forces she has unleashed until, by the end, she is the very opposite of a saint. The all-powerful Gilles, meanwhile, although writer, director, producer, great lord, and lead actor is revealed to be the true innocent, the true victim of his own devices and desires. Rather than master manipulator and monster, Gilles' destiny is discovered, by him and us at the same time, to be that of an innocent consort.

In this assessment of Gilles de Rais, Clark is admirably prescient. In a 1992 retrial of de Rais' case in France, the court found the accusations of mass rape and murder completely unfounded in evidence and declared him a victim of a conspiracy and innocent of all charges. While this finding is a compliment to the hypothesis of Clark's play, it also, more to the point, reveals the importance still invested in the subjects and issues of the play by contemporary European historians and jurists. Something *strange* happened, something that provokes and demands attention to this day.

In grounding her Jehanne in the Old Religion, and conceiving her play as a recreation of sacrificial drama — the practice of many Old Religions, Clark risks being tarred with the aura of New Age magicalism. But theatre is a searingly humane art form. It brings any god down to earth, and in *Jehanne of the Witches* it allows Clark to retain her distance and irony — Jehanne's Voices are so correct — while revealing the primal battle/ballet between man and woman.

Her conclusions are not nice. Underneath all the words of power, visions, and illusions, a bloody deal-making is going on. The play shows its truest insight by fusing this visceral, erotic dance of the individuals with the consequences of the mythic memory of history.

History as illusion, a theatre of legend which transforms events, is not a new idea, but in *Jehanne of the Witches* it provides for Clark a spiritual and intellectual mystery play — complete with comforting circularity — and an opportunity to expose the sacrificial ritual at the heart of theatre itself.

If life is a play in which no one survives, and theatre is a way of asking why and what for, history and faith, which provide the comfort and identity of humanity, must be questioned. by exploring the theatre of both history and faith as she does, Sally Clark casts new light on both, and challenges us to look more deeply into the true power of each.

It is dangerous, if not impossible, to expect any work of art to provide a solution to any problem, social or spiritual. That's not its function. A play is a proposition, a hypothetical universe, from which inferences can be drawn and instruction taken. Few good plays *prove* anything. Certainly this play does not *prove* Jeanne d'Arc was a witch, nor does it prove that a new and trendy age of paganism is upon us. Instead, the play reminds us that there are more things in heaven and earth than we understand and the primal dialectic between the male and the female of the species, regardless of our sexual preferences, is a defining dynamic of our existence.

Also, there are some good jokes.

Clarke Rogers
Flesherton, November, 1993

Playwright's Foreword

Preface to the Play

This play is not like my earlier plays. It came about partly as a dare and partly out of my own desire to write something different. At the time, I was bereft of ideas so Clarke Rogers issued me a challenge — write a play about positive female power. My thoughts instantly flew to Joan of Arc. In my reading, I discovered that witchcraft / Satanism was an invention of the Christian Church. While the Church was trying to establish itself, the populace still worshipped the pagan gods - primarily the Moon Goddess. The Church couldn't obliterate Goddess worship so it usurped the pagan shrines and replaced Goddess worship with "Mary" worship.

Joan of Arc falls on the seam of this conflict. She was one of the first witches to be burned at the stake. Jehanne la Pucelle was her original title. The Church renamed her Jeanne d'Arc. "La Pucelle" is the title given to the female head of a coven. I felt that by putting the "h" back in her name, I was reclaiming something that had been lost.

In the translation from pagan to Christian history, someone else has been lost to us: Gilles de Rais (1404 - 1440), a man we only know through the fairy tale Bluebeard — reputedly a black magician who murdered 200 boys. Bluebeard and Joan of Arc were best friends. Fighting side-by-side in battle, he saved her life twice and emerged Marshall of France. After Joan's death, Gilles staged a pageant about her victory at Orleans. Some historians claim that Gilles de Rais is the founder of modern French theatre. His *Mystery of the Siege of Orleans* is one of the first plays on a secular subject. Most unusual was Gilles' presentation of the play. He staged the play on sets around the entire town of Orleans. People followed the action from set to set. Gilles de

Rais was a scientist and an alchemist. He may or may not have been a mass murderer.

The play is historically accurate. You might not agree with my interpretation but the events are true.

Preface to a production

This play is about Magic, Truth and Illusion: three themes to be juggled in the air and kept aloft. The play-within-a-play structure is simply a plot device — a magician's trick. Please don't centre the entire play around it. A good magician dazzles his audience. He doesn't explain the tricks as he performs them.

So, the first 40 minutes of the play should be the Joan of Arc story. It should not be Gilles de Rais' acting company putting on a play. If you focus on 15th-Century acting styles and a church-basement look, the audience will simply think it's a bad play and will not be with you when the play flips out of Joan's story.

A note to the actor playing Jehanne: You are Joan of Arc for the first 40 minutes of the play and for a great deal of the second act. Play it as Joan of Arc. Don't play it as the actor François playing Joan of Arc. When you are cast in a play, you wouldn't play yourself playing a part. The change from Jehanne to François should be as quick and sudden as a magician's trick. Think of Jehanne and François as two separate and very different people and you flip from one to the other.

This note applies to all the actors. You are who you are in the scene. For example: the young Gilles in Joan's story is very different from the older actor-manager Gilles. Play the scene, not the play-within-the-play.

Sally Clark
Toronto, November 1993

Acknowledgements

The writing of *Jehanne of the Witches* was generously assisted by the Laidlaw Foundation and the Ontario Arts Council. The play was commissioned by Clarke Rogers in July, 1986. It was developed and workshopped at Theatre Passe Muraille in November, 1987. The author would like to thank Clarke Rogers for his invaluable help in developing the script. Thanks also to Maja Ardal for her contributions to the project.

I would particularly like to thank Urjo Kareda for rescuing the play from the confines of my bottom drawer and for his encouragement, generosity, and expertise in seeing it through to production.

Jehanne of the Witches was first published in *Theatrum*, April/May issue, 1990, #18.

PRODUCTION HISTORY

Jehanne of the Witches was first produced at the Tarragon Theatre, Toronto, November, 1989, with the following cast:

JEHANNE	*JoAnn McIntyre*
GILLES DE RAIS	*Sky Gilbert*
VOICE1, MICHAEL, POULENGY, FOOL, MINGUET, BASTARD, WHORE, MOTHER	*Maria Ricossa*
VOICE 2, CATHERINE, DE BAUDRICOURT LA HIRE, WHORE, MOTHER	*Jennifer Dean*
VOICE 3, MARGARET, ISABELLE	*Terry Tweed*
CHARLES, GOD, BISHOP	*Patrick Brymer*
GEORGE, BISHOP CAUCHON	*Ted Johns*
PRIEST (PIERRE) PASQUEREL ARCHBISHOP, VILLAGE PRIEST	*John Blackwood*

Directed by Clarke Rogers.
Set design by Dorian Clarke.
Costume design by Denyse Karn.
Lighting design by Paul Mathiesen.
Original music and sound designed by David Jaggs.
Stage manager - Candace Burley.

THE CHARACTERS

JEHANNE THE MAID

GILLES DE RAIS

VOICE 1, (THE ARCHANGEL MICHAEL), also plays POULENGY, FOOL, MINGUET, THE BASTARD OF ORLEANS, WHORE 1 and a MOTHER

VOICE 2, (SAINT CATHERINE) also plays DE BAUDRICOURT, LA HIRE, WHORE 2 and a MOTHER

VOICE 3, (SAINT MARGARET) also plays ISABELLE, Jehanne's mother

CHARLES THE DAUPHIN, also plays GOD and a BISHOP

GEORGE DE TREMOUILLE, also plays BISHOP CAUCHON

PRIEST (PIERRE), also plays VILLAGE PRIEST, ARCHBISHOP OF RHEIMS, and PASQUEREL

Act One, Scene One

Domremy, France. 1422. Day. A young girl is staring at a large tree. Sound of church bells. The girl starts up as if to go, then changes her mind and approaches the tree nervously. While she approaches the tree, three women's VOICES are heard. The three women are behind a scrim, near the tree. They are invisible to the audience. One woman is young. The other two women are older. They are the three VOICES known as MICHAEL, CATHERINE and MARGARET, respectively. The church bells are still ringing.

VOICE 2   What's that awful noise?

VOICE 3   Mass. The Christians are at it again.

VOICE 2   It's deafening. Why is it so loud? I don't remember it being so loud.

VOICE 3   They're taking over.

VOICE 2   It's insidious.

The bells stop.

VOICE 1	I've nothing really against the Christians but it seems that ever since they defined reality, the only people who see us now are lunatics.
VOICE 2	People have stopped listening.
VOICE 3	We don't exist for them, anymore.
VOICE 1	I can feel myself fading. Not only can they not see us, but I can't see them very clearly. Did you know there is a young girl stepping on your toe?
VOICE 2	I don't feel anything.
VOICE 1	Exactly. If she were to come any closer, it might be the end of us.
	The girl looks down at the ground and moves in to pick up something. The women gasp. The girl reels backward. Church bells ring. The girl turns and stares in the direction of the voices.
VOICES	*(mixed in with church bells in echoing manner)* Jehanne Jehanne Jehanne!
	The church bells stop.
JEHANNE	Who are you? How do you know my name?
	Lights up on VOICE 1.
VOICE 2	She has some of our power.
JEHANNE	Pardon?
VOICE 2	She can hear me.
VOICE 1	Can you see anyone else, Jehanne?
JEHANNE	No. Just you.
VOICE 2	Let's get her to do something.

VOICE 3	Yes.
JEHANNE	I hear voices. But they're all mixed up.
VOICE 1	One thing at a time. We're confusing her.
JEHANNE	My head hurts. I can't see you, anymore. Where are you?
VOICE 1	We're in the light.

JEHANNE peers at the light.

VOICE 1	Calm yourself, Jehanne. You can't see us because you're afraid. Breathe deeply and slowly. Don't close your eyes. Look up slowly into the light.
JEHANNE	*(looking up, seeing VOICE 1 and making a curtsey)* Archangel Michael.
MICHAEL	Why do you call us that?
JEHANNE	That's who you are, isn't it? You look like all the pictures I've seen.
MICHAEL	Are there many pictures of us?
JEHANNE	Oh yes. You're in Mary's cave.
MICHAEL	Mary's cave.
JEHANNE	The shrine of the Blessed Virgin.
MICHAEL	Oh yes, of course. That cave.
JEHANNE	And there are all those old coins with your picture on it.
MICHAEL	Roman coins?
JEHANNE	No. Old coins. *(curtseying again)* I'm honoured, Archangel, that you've come all the way from Heaven to talk to me. It must be very important. Is there something I can do?

VOICE 3	Good. Now's our chance.
VOICE 2	We have an important message for you.
VOICE 3	Pay close attention.
JEHANNE	Yes.
MICHAEL	Be good.
VOICES 2, 3 & JEHANNE	That's it?
MICHAEL	That's it.

Pause.

MICHAEL	What's wrong, Jehanne?
JEHANNE	What if you're a demon pretending to be the Archangel?
MICHAEL	Would a demon tell you to be good?
JEHANNE	No. But the Devil might. He's very cunning.
MICHAEL	What's a Devil?
JEHANNE	The Devil. He's a fallen angel. Except he's got horns and a tail. And he tempts people.

VOICE 2 and 3 laugh.

JEHANNE	I don't see what's so funny. I think my parents worship the Devil. But I'm not sure. They don't do evil things. The priests say that Devil worshippers do evil things.
MICHAEL	Look at us, Jehanne. Do you see any horns on us?
JEHANNE	No.
MICHAEL	Pay no attention to the priests. There's no Devil.

JEHANNE   No?

MICHAEL   But there is evil. And you must be on guard against it. So, Jehanne...

JEHANNE   Yes?

MICHAEL   Be good.

JEHANNE   Yes.

MICHAEL   And go to Mass every day.

VOICE 2   Why are you telling her that?

JEHANNE   My mother thinks I go too often.

VOICE 2   She's right.

MICHAEL   Do it anyway. Oh, and Jehanne.

JEHANNE   Yes.

MICHAEL   Don't tell anyone you were talking to us.

JEHANNE   Not even my mother?

VOICE 3   Especially not your mother.

JEHANNE   Why not?

MICHAEL   Your mother will get too excited.

VOICE 2   We don't want anything to interfere with your mission.

JEHANNE   My mission?

MICHAEL   Yes, Jehanne. You have a mission. You are going to do something very very important.

JEHANNE   What is it?

MICHAEL   We can't tell you, now. We must leave. Don't tell anyone you saw us. You must keep it a secret.

JEHANNE   Why?

MICHAEL   Keeping the secret will increase the power.

JEHANNE   What power?

VOICES   The power growing within you.

The VOICES disappear.

JEHANNE   Michael? *(looking around for them)*

Scene Two

JEHANNE and her mother are doing laundry.

JEHANNE Maman, where do you go in the middle of the night?

ISABELLE It was a new moon.

JEHANNE Yes.

ISABELLE That's the time to start things. You want the crops to do well, don't you?

JEHANNE Yes.

ISABELLE Well, we have to go out and talk to the Moon so she doesn't forget about us. There used to be a lot of gods and you could ask them to do things for you. Now there's only one and He doesn't have time to look after everyone. The Moon. She's much more use to us than God is. You can talk to the Moon. And in the day, you can talk to the King of Heaven as He travels across the sky.

JEHANNE How do you get the gods to do things for you? Hauviette said that in the spring, everyone goes to the tree and they take off all their clothes and they pee on each other. Is that true?

ISABELLE	No. I think Hauviette is confusing that with something else.
JEHANNE	Well, what do they do then?
ISABELLE	When you're older, I'll tell you.
JEHANNE	Why not now?
ISABELLE	It's not time. It won't be long, though.

Church bells ring.

JEHANNE	I have to go.
ISABELLE	Promise me one thing, Jeanette. Never say their prayer.
JEHANNE	But Maman, why? It's harmless. Saying "Our Father who art in Heaven" doesn't mean I believe it.
ISABELLE	The King of Heaven is nobody's father. If enough people say anything enough times, it becomes true. I don't ask much from you. I simply ask you never to say that prayer.
JEHANNE	Yes, Maman. I'm going to be late. *(kissing her and leaving)*

Scene Three

JEHANNE and the PRIEST. JEHANNE is in confession.

PRIEST   You wish to make a confession?

JEHANNE   Bless me, Father, for I have nothing to confess.

Long pause.

PRIEST   You are in a state of grace, then? It is presumptuous to think that you are.

JEHANNE   No, Father. I do not presume anything. But I haven't sinned lately so I have nothing to confess.

PRIEST   If you are free of sin, then you are assuming yourself to be in a state of grace. Only God can put you in a state of grace. Your presumption itself is a sin.

JEHANNE   Which sin, Father?

PRIEST   The sin of pride, my child. So, we begin again. You wish to make a confession?

JEHANNE   Bless me, Father, for I have sinned.

PRIEST   What is this sin you have committed?

JEHANNE	The sin of pride, Father.
PRIEST	How have you committed this sin, my child?
JEHANNE	I am proud because I have nothing to confess.
PRIEST	You are proud because you think you have nothing to confess.
JEHANNE	That's what I said, Father.
PRIEST	No, my child. You did not say that.
JEHANNE	I'm sorry, Father. I meant to say that. Father, I have something to tell you. I don't know whether this is a sin or not.
PRIEST	What is it, my child?
JEHANNE	Father, the other day, I was outside in the woods and I heard—
MICHAEL	*(voice off, whispering)* No.
JEHANNE	I heard—
MICHAEL	No!
PRIEST	Yes, my child.
JEHANNE	I heard my mother calling me and I pretended not to hear her.
PRIEST	Why didn't you go to her, my child?
JEHANNE	I didn't feel like it, Father.
PRIEST	That is a minor transgression, my child. It would be more serious if it was your father calling you. We will absolve you just the same.
JEHANNE	Thank you, Father.

Act One / 31

PRIEST   (*absolving her*) Misereatur tui omnipotens Deus et, dismissis peccátis tuis, perdúcat te ad vitam aetérnam. Amen.

JEHANNE leaves the confession. The PRIEST hurries out of his booth and comes up beside her.

PRIEST   Do you ever go to the Ladies' Tree, Jehanne?

JEHANNE   What tree, Father?

PRIEST   The large tree in the grove. You know the one I mean.

JEHANNE   I like to walk in the forest, Father. God made the forests for us to walk in.

PRIEST   Do you ever see people dancing around the Tree, Jehanne?

JEHANNE   Children dance there on May Day. You knew that, didn't you, Father?

PRIEST   Yes. I knew that. But other times. At night.

JEHANNE   Father, why would I go to the forest at night. I would get lost.

PRIEST   I'm not suggesting that you go to the Tree, Jehanne. I'm simply asking if you've seen people there.

JEHANNE   I would have to be there to see people, wouldn't I, Father.

PRIEST   So, you've never been near the Tree, Jehanne?

JEHANNE   Father, what would happen if God asked someone like me to do something for Him?

PRIEST   God wouldn't talk to someone like you.

JEHANNE   He'd send angels down, instead?

PRIEST   No.

JEHANNE   But He sent angels to the saints, didn't He?

PRIEST   Because they were saints.

JEHANNE   But were they saints when they were growing up?

PRIEST   We mustn't confuse the saints with people who think they see visions from Heaven. Because not all visions are from Heaven. Some are evil. The people who see visions come to us and we decide whether their visions are evil or not.

JEHANNE   How can you tell?

PRIEST   There's a scent to a vision from Heaven. It is like nothing on earth. Sweet and fragrant. The Devil cannot disguise his bad scent. That is how you can know evil people. They love bad scents. The smell of decaying matter delights them. They always look as though they are smelling something quite revolting and enjoying it thoroughly.

JEHANNE   What about dogs?

PRIEST   *(annoyed)* What about dogs!

JEHANNE   Dogs like bad scents.

PRIEST   Yes. And they are frequently witches' familiars. But they are merely beasts so they are not to blame if a demon inhabits them. Demons can take any shape. Like the Ladies' Tree. I'm going to go tonight and see for myself.

JEHANNE   That's very brave of you, Father.

PRIEST   Brave. Why?

JEHANNE   Any man who goes to the Ladies' Tree at night is cursed.

Act One / 33

PRIEST   What sort of curse?

JEHANNE   He is turned into a woman.

PRIEST   Who told you that? You don't really think—

JEHANNE   I don't know Father. People here say it happened. *(leaving)*

>*A nobleman enters. He is BARON GILLES DE RAIS, Marshall of France.*

GILLES   Have you got any more boys for me? That last one didn't work out.

PRIEST   What was wrong with him? He was beautiful. An angel.

GILLES   Ah — he couldn't sing.

PRIEST   He has a magnificent voice. A cry to Heaven.

GILLES   Voice is turning. Agony to listen to. Sounds like a crow in heat. My Chapel of Holy Innocents needs new blood.

PRIEST   I'll put the word out.

GILLES   Can't you pick one out for me?

PRIEST   No. It's too many. You want too many boys.

GILLES   *(handing him some money)* Surely, you can find one.

PRIEST   They're easy enough to find. They're clamouring at your gates.

GILLES   *(handing him more money)* I prefer it when you find them for me. You have exquisite taste.

PRIEST   I don't think we should see each other, anymore. Rumours—

GILLES	Rumours?
PRIEST	The Nightingale. What happened to him?
GILLES	Nothing. He's fine. You chose well, Pierre.
PRIEST	Do you mind calling me by my title.
GILLES	Am I now "Marshall"?
PRIEST	Yes. I haven't seen the Nightingale for three months. He was my prize boy. It's not like him. I can't believe he'd be so ungrateful. His family keeps asking me for news.
GILLES	He leads a different life now. He's busy. The choir is touring the provinces this month. Fame or family. You can't have both. They should be very proud of their son.
PRIEST	They are, Marshall. They would like to see him to tell him so.
GILLES	When he gets back, I'll send him over to visit.
PRIEST	They would appreciate that.
GILLES	So, you'll find me another? *(pulling out more money)* Father?
PRIEST	Oh, all right. *(taking the money)*

They leave in opposite directions.

Act One / 35

Scene Four

JEHANNE, alone in the forest. MICHAEL and VOICE 2 are watching her. She does not see them.

MICHAEL Jehanne.

VOICE 2 Jehanne the Maid.

JEHANNE gasps.

MICHAEL Did we startle you?

JEHANNE Yes.

MICHAEL You should be used to us by now.

JEHANNE Michael, why is it that I can see you and nobody else can?

VOICE 2 I'd like to know why she can't see me.

MICHAEL You haven't told anyone, have you?

JEHANNE No. But why—

MICHAEL It's a gift. Don't dwell on such things. If you become too aware of your powers, you won't be able to see me, anymore.

VOICE 2	We don't have much time.
JEHANNE	Time for what?
VOICE 2	Good. She heard me. Jehanne the Maid. The King of Heaven has a job for you.
MICHAEL	*(to Voice 2)* I don't think this is a wise idea.
VOICE 2	Nothing ventured, nothing gained.
JEHANNE	Michael, is that voice one of Heaven's saints?
VOICE 2	Yes.
JEHANNE	Which one?
VOICE 2	Guess.
JEHANNE	Saint Catherine?
CATHERINE	Dead on. Now listen, carefully, Jehanne. You are going to save France. You will restore the Dauphin Charles to his rightful throne and France will be united under him.
JEHANNE	How will I do this?
MICHAEL	Good question.
CATHERINE	You will wear arms and become head of the King of Heaven's army. Our army will drive the English out of France.
JEHANNE	But I know nothing of riding or fighting.
CATHERINE	Michael will guide you. *(to MICHAEL)* You're going to have to take over. I'm feeling faint. The sacrifice. *(withdrawing)*
MICHAEL	We require a sacrifice from you. This sacrifice will give you the power.
JEHANNE	What is it?

Act One / 37

MICHAEL   You must remain a virgin.

JEHANNE   Good. I don't want to get married.

MICHAEL   It's very important that you retain your virginity. Men might try and take it from you. Dress in men's clothes. You will pass as one of them and will not arouse their lust.

JEHANNE   I'm really going to be in the army?!

MICHAEL   You're going to be head of it. So, protect and defend your virginity at all costs.

JEHANNE   Why is it so important?

MICHAEL   Virginity gives you clarity. If you lose it, you won't be able to see or hear me. It takes many years to reach that state of clarity. We don't have that much time.

JEHANNE   How much time do we have?

MICHAEL   Seven years since the time you first saw me.

JEHANNE   I'm sixteen now. That's only four years.

MICHAEL   It's enough time if we start right away. First, you have to see the Dauphin. You will have to do that through one of his officers. Robert de Beaudricourt is stationed in Vaucouleurs. You will have to see him first. He won't want to talk to you. He'll think you're mad. So, you will have to be persistent.

JEHANNE   Michael?

MICHAEL   Yes.

JEHANNE   I'm not mad, am I?

MICHAEL   Jehanne the Maid, don't ask silly questions. Your mother's coming. Tell her that you want to go to Vaucouleurs.

Jehanne of the Witches / 38

JEHANNE	I can't ask her like that. She'll want to know why.
MICHAEL	Your cousin is pregnant. Say you'd like to help with the birth.
ISABELLE	*(entering)* Jeanette! There you are! I have to talk to you. It's very important. Your father had a vision.

JEHANNE looks at MICHAEL.

MICHAEL	*(shrugging)* I was trying to talk to him.
ISABELLE	Jeanette. Pay attention. These things don't happen every day. He's very upset about it.
JEHANNE	Did he see an angel?
ISABELLE	Good Heavens no! It wasn't a vision, exactly. It was really a dream. But it was very vivid. And he woke up extremely worried about you. You don't know any soldiers, do you?
JEHANNE	No. Why?
ISABELLE	You don't talk to them, do you? If they walk by on the road?
JEHANNE	No. You told me not to. What's all this about?
ISABELLE	Well, your father dreamed that you'd gone off to live with the soldiers.
JEHANNE	Oh.
ISABELLE	Well...actually, he dreamed that you'd become a camp follower.
MICHAEL	Garbled.
JEHANNE	Pardon?
ISABELLE	Oh-well-you-know, one of those women...

Act One / 39

MICHAEL	They always get the message wrong.
	JEHANNE looks puzzled.
ISABELLE	A whore.
MICHAEL	You say one thing and it comes out completely the opposite.
JEHANNE	What?! Father thought I'd become a whore. That's awful. I'd never do that! Never!
ISABELLE	It's all so preposterous. You'd never be a camp follower. You're not attractive enough for one thing.
JEHANNE	I'm not?
ISABELLE	You don't have that sort of look about you.
JEHANNE	What sort of look is it?
ISABELLE	The less you know about that, the better. Your father's in a state and insists you get married immediately.
MICHAEL & JEHANNE	*(together)* You can't get married! I can't get married!
ISABELLE	I agree. You're too young. But you can be engaged for a few years. We'll have to find one of our own people. I'll not have you marrying a Christian. They beat their wives.
JEHANNE	How do they become camp followers? Do they get tempted into it? Does the Devil disguise himself and lure them into it?
MICHAEL	You're so suspicious, Jehanne.
ISABELLE	The priests again! What is this devil they keep talking about?

JEHANNE	I think you meet him in the forest, Maman.
ISABELLE	*(examining JEHANNE)* We meet with the wood spirits. There is no devil that I know of. Your blood hasn't run yet, has it?
JEHANNE	Maman, do you see anything over there? *(pointing to MICHAEL)*
ISABELLE	Don't be embarrassed, Jeanette. We've talked about this, before. You're changing into a woman. See, you have breasts. Nice ones, too.
JEHANNE	Maman —
ISABELLE	So easy to embarrass.
JEHANNE	Maman, very strange things are happening to me.
MICHAEL	If you tell her, you'll never see me again.
ISABELLE	It's natural for your age. Difficult time. Power time.
MICHAEL	France needs you, Jehanne.
JEHANNE	Power time?
ISABELLE	Yes. You have an immense amount of power at this age. But you're all bottled up. We should get your blood flowing. That's probably why you feel strange.
JEHANNE	What would happen if it didn't flow?
ISABELLE	It always flows.
JEHANNE	But if it didn't.
ISABELLE	Then, you'd be a creature apart.
JEHANNE	*(to MICHAEL)* Is that why you can talk to me?

Act One / 41

ISABELLE	We've always been able to talk, Jeanette.
JEHANNE	What sort of creature?
ISABELLE	Oh...I don't know. You'd be a girl but you'd have a woman's power — without the tempering that goes along with it.
MICHAEL	You want the power, don't you?
ISABELLE	We'll be meeting tonight. I'll ask the Maid to prepare something special for you.
JEHANNE	Why do you call Frances the Maid? She's married and has five children.
ISABELLE	That's her title. Like the Dauphin.
JEHANNE	Do people always call him the Dauphin? Or can they call him Charles?
MICHAEL	We'll get to that later. First things first. Tell her you want to go to Vaucouleurs.
ISABELLE	Only if they know him well.
MICHAEL	Tell her.
JEHANNE	I want to go to Vaucouleurs. Visit my uncle and his wife.
ISABELLE	Pardon me?
JEHANNE	Aunt Marie is pregnant and I'd like to help her with the birthing.
ISABELLE	How did you know she was pregnant?
JEHANNE	You told me.
ISABELLE	I did? I don't remember.
JEHANNE	So, it's settled, then. I'll pack my things. *(starting to leave)*

ISABELLE *(looking confused)* It's settled? *(pause, looking at JEHANNE)* Jeanette, are you all right?

JEHANNE Couldn't be better, Maman. It's my Power time.

Scene Five

ROBERT DE BAUDRICOURT's offices in Vaucouleurs. He is with his officer, POULENGY who is played by MICHAEL. DE BAUDRICOURT is played by CATHERINE.

BAUDRICOURT France is teeming with mystics and prophets — all claiming to be her saviour. Making a damn good living at it, too. Let me tell you, Poully, I've met more convincing mystics in my time. This one's so ordinary. She's a big lumpy farm girl. She's about as mystical as a block of wood.

POULENGY I believe her, Seigneur.

BAUDRICOURT Then, you're an even bigger fool than I thought you were.

JEHANNE enters. She is wearing a red dress. She bows to DE BAUDRICOURT.

JEHANNE Seigneur de Baudricourt.

BAUDRICOURT Poully!

POULENGY Please, just hear her out, Seigneur.

JEHANNE	You must let me see the Dauphin. He should not engage in battle, yet, because my Lord will not give him help till mid-Lent. You are planning a battle, now. It will not go well.
BAUDRICOURT	Another goddamn prophecy.
JEHANNE	Please do not swear, Seigneur. It's very vulgar. I must see the Dauphin. We must save the kingdom of France.
BAUDRICOURT	What does your Lord care about France?
JEHANNE	The kingdom belongs to my Lord.
BAUDRICOURT	I thought it belonged to the Dauphin.
JEHANNE	Oh no, my Lord wants the Dauphin to become King so he can look after it on behalf of my Lord. I must lead the army into victory and crown the Dauphin. And if you won't give me an escort, I will go myself.
BAUDRICOURT	Who is your Lord?
JEHANNE	*(pausing)* The King of Heaven.
BAUDRICOURT	God, you mean.
JEHANNE	I mean the King of Heaven.
BAUDRICOURT	How does your Lord give you these instructions?

JEHANNE pauses.

BAUDRICOURT	Well?
JEHANNE	I was told it was all right to tell you. But no other. *(looking at POULENGY)* You must go.
BAUDRICOURT	*(as POULENGY starts to leave)* You have the temerity to dismiss one of my men?!
JEHANNE	Do you want to know or not?

BAUDRICOURT   Poully. Dismissed!

POULENGY exits.

JEHANNE   You must swear never to reveal this to anyone.

BAUDRICOURT   I swear by God.

JEHANNE   You must swear by Mary. You were brought up by Mary. You must swear by Her.

BAUDRICOURT   How did you know —

JEHANNE   Swear.

BAUDRICOURT   I swear by Mary never to reveal what you tell me.

JEHANNE   The Voice gives me my instructions.

BAUDRICOURT   The Voice?

JEHANNE   Yes. The voice of the Archangel Michael.

BAUDRICOURT   Can you hear the voice clearly?

JEHANNE   As clearly as I can hear you.

BAUDRICOURT   What if it's the voice of a demon.

JEHANNE   Your voice is more like a demon than my Voice. *(sniffing)* And you smell.

BAUDRICOURT   Why you impudent bitch!

JEHANNE   You do swear a lot, Seigneur.

BAUDRICOURT   Do you hear your Voice at night or in the daytime?

JEHANNE   In the day. I see Michael in the light of day.

BAUDRICOURT   What does he look like?

JEHANNE	I am not at liberty to discuss these matters.
BAUDRICOURT	You're from Lorraine. That region is suspect. The Old Religion is practised there.
JEHANNE	You should know that. You were brought up in the old ways.
BAUDRICOURT	How did you know that?
JEHANNE	Your mother's name is Catherine. You were born with a caul. It is buried under the paving stone at the back of her house.
BAUDRICOURT	Enough. Did your Voice tell you this?
JEHANNE	Yes. And more besides. But I don't have time to tell you your life history. I want Poulengy and de Metz to accompany me to Chinon. I'll need a suit of men's clothing.
BAUDRICOURT	Why can't you go as you are?
JEHANNE	My Voice tells me that these clothes are not appropriate. I will arouse men's lust.
BAUDRICOURT	I don't think you need to worry about that.
JEHANNE	I think I do.

Scene Six

JEHANNE and MICHAEL. JEHANNE is wearing a red dress. MICHAEL hands her a tunic, doublet and hose.

JEHANNE I'll just put them on underneath my dress. Just to get used to it. *(putting them on)*

MICHAEL Take off your dress, Jehanne.

JEHANNE Must I?

MICHAEL Yes.

JEHANNE *(pulling dress off, donning tunic and walking tentatively)* I feel so...I feel naked.

MICHAEL You must learn to use your body. Begin with the legs.

JEHANNE What do you mean? I can walk.

MICHAEL You must learn to walk as men walk. In long clean strides. Imitate one of your brothers.

JEHANNE *(walking with exaggerated boldness)* Is this a sin?

MICHAEL Why?

JEHANNE I feel as though it's a sin. I feel—

MICHAEL   Wanton?

JEHANNE   Yes.

MICHAEL   You're the Maid. La Pucelle. The wanton virgin. *(laughing, then suddenly staring at her)* There's still something wrong. Oh yes, the hair. *(pulling out scissors)* It's got to come off.

JEHANNE   Oh no, please. I love my hair. I've got nice hair.

MICHAEL   You'll never be pretty, Jehanne. But you could be beautiful if you were bold enough.

JEHANNE   You're just saying that.

MICHAEL   Yes. I am. See that bowl over there. Put it on top of your head and cut around it.

> *JEHANNE puts bowl on head and cuts around it. MICHAEL walks around her while she is doing this. JEHANNE takes the bowl off. Her hair is cut short like a page boy.*

JEHANNE   *(fingering it)* It feels strange. *(shaking her head)* Lighter.

MICHAEL   Yes. Hair can be a burden. *(pulling long hair off head to reveal short cropped head)*

> *JEHANNE gasps.*

MICHAEL   *(laughing)* Be bold, Jehanne. You are not Jeanette, anymore. Take your red dress and burn it. *(pulling out a lighter and a candle, then lighting the candle)*

JEHANNE   *(staring at the lighter)* How did you—

MICHAEL   Burn it. *(handing her the candle and disappearing)*

JEHANNE looks at the dress. She blows out the candle and folds up the dress very carefully.

Scene Seven

Chinon. Anteroom to the court. JEHANNE is waiting. MICHAEL is dressed as a courtier. A large fat man rushes by. His name is GEORGE DE LA TREMOUILLE. He stops, looks at JEHANNE and goes up to MICHAEL.

GEORGE Hasn't she gone home yet? I told her to go home.

MICHAEL She won't leave, Sire.

JEHANNE Seigneur de Baudricourt has given me an escort.

GEORGE *(to JEHANNE)* I don't believe I was addressing you.

JEHANNE The Dauphin will be very upset when he learns that you have prevented me from seeing him. The Dauphin is expecting me.

MICHAEL It's true, Sire. One of de Baudricourt's men told him she was here.

GEORGE Oh. All right, then. *(to JEHANNE)* You have five minutes.

JEHANNE starts to go in. GEORGE pulls her back.

GEORGE   Not so fast. You will wait here to be summoned.

JEHANNE   How long?

GEORGE ignores her and leaves.

Scene Eight

> *Chinon. The voices CATHERINE and MARGARET are ladies of the court. The PRIEST is dressed as The ARCHBISHOP OF RHEIMS. GILLES DE RAIS is seated on the DAUPHIN's throne. GEORGE stands nearby. CHARLES THE DAUPHIN is dressed in shabby clothes. He is standing by the LADIES OF THE COURT and trying to look inconspicuous. JEHANNE is led into the room by MICHAEL the courtier. The LADIES OF THE COURT titter.*

CATHERINE What is that?

MARGARET Is it a boy? Is it a girl? Or is it just ugly! *(laughing)*

> *JEHANNE looks at GILLES DE RAIS and takes a step toward the throne. Everyone is silent. JEHANNE pauses and looks around the room. She sees the DAUPHIN and stares at him.*

MICHAEL It is rude to keep the Dauphin waiting, Mademoiselle.

Act One / 53

>*JEHANNE goes to the DAUPHIN and drops a curtsey. Someone in the crowd gasps softly.*

JEHANNE Noble Dauphin, I am Jehanne the Maid. The King of Heaven sends me to you with a message.

CHARLES You had better address yourself to the Dauphin. He is on his throne. *(pointing to GILLES)*

JEHANNE He looks more like a Dauphin than you do, Sire. He is better dressed and he's probably more intelligent, but it is you I have come to serve.

>*THE LADIES OF THE COURT giggle.*

CHARLES If I were the Dauphin, I'd cut off your head for saying that. But since I'm not the Dauphin, consider yourself lucky.

JEHANNE The Dauphin I serve is a kind, just man.

MICHAEL Then, you've come to the wrong court.

GILLES Insolence! There will be no insolence in our court! We are as the Maid describes us.

JEHANNE The Dauphin is as I described him, Monsieur. I can't speak for you.

GILLES So, you think we would chop off your head?

JEHANNE I think you're capable of it.

CHARLES Mademoiselle is a good judge of character.

GEORGE Send this creature back to the woods!

GILLES You had a message for us, Mademoiselle?

JEHANNE I am Jehanne the Maid.

GEORGE You are nothing to us, Mademoiselle.

JEHANNE	My message is meant for the Dauphin only.
GEORGE	He is over here. *(gesturing to GILLES)*
JEHANNE	Then, I will address the court. *(to CHARLES)* You will regret it. Parts of my message are very personal. *(bowing and kneeling to CHARLES)* O Noble Dauphin, the King of Heaven has sent me to save France. I must lead the army. We will raise the siege of Orleans. Then we will anoint and crown you at Rheims and all France will be united.
CHARLES	Well, that sounds easy. Shall we do it this morning or do you want to have lunch first?
ARCHBISHOP	Wait just a minute! That's my cathedral she's talking about.
CHARLES	*(to JEHANNE)* The Archbishop of Rheims. *(to ARCHBISHOP)* Really, your Eminence, calm down. You're never in Rheims, anyway.
ARCHBISHOP	She's disposing of my property! *(to JEHANNE)* You're from the Old Region, aren't you?
JEHANNE	I'm from Domremy, Lorraine.
ARCHBISHOP	Exactly! She's a witch. *(to JEHANNE)* Why are you wearing men's clothes?
JEHANNE	I dress as a man so I will not arouse their lust.
ARCHBISHOP	It is the witches' custom to cross-dress. Are you a virgin?
JEHANNE	Yes. Of course.
ARCHBISHOP	A likely story.
JEHANNE	I don't understand.

Act One / 55

GILLES If you are a virgin, you have not had intercourse. Therefore, you have not had intercourse with the Devil. Therefore, you are not a witch.

ARCHBISHOP And don't think we'll take your word for it. If she's staying, she will have to be examined.

GILLES Better keep your virga intacta.

JEHANNE *(to CHARLES)* The King of Heaven heard your special prayer — the one you made on All Saints Day.

ARCHBISHOP That is the Witches' New Year.

JEHANNE *(to CHARLES)* I wasn't praying on that day, Sire. You were.

GILLES Would you please look at us when you're talking to us.

JEHANNE *(ignoring GILLES)* The King of Heaven sent me to reassure you that you are the true heir to the throne.

CHARLES Well, that's very flattering. I'm really just a lowly courtier, but it's always nice to know that one can rise in this world.

JEHANNE Oh please, Sire. This charade is tiresome. Shall I tell the whole court that you're afraid of going mad.

GILLES The question is: has it happened already?

CHARLES *(to GILLES)* Sir! You go too far!

JEHANNE Sire, the King of Heaven assures you that you won't go mad.

CHARLES *(clasping hands in prayer)* Oh, thank you.

JEHANNE However, you are weak and snivelling and a disgrace to your blood.

CHARLES	What!
JEHANNE	That's what he said, Sire. But you needn't worry. I'm here to take care of that.

> *CHARLES draws JEHANNE aside. The COURT tries to listen. CHARLES glares at them. The COURT talks quietly amongst itself.*

CHARLES	*(faltering)* Being the true King, then we are required for the Sacrifice.
JEHANNE	The Sacrifice shall be made so that you may rule.
CHARLES	How long will we rule?
JEHANNE	For many years.
CHARLES	So, we are not to be the Sacrifice?
JEHANNE	No, Sire.
CHARLES	Did the King of Heaven say who was to be the Sacrifice?
JEHANNE	No, Sire.

> *CHARLES notices that people are trying to listen to his conversation.*

CHARLES	*(loudly)* You're sure he didn't say Baron de Rais was to be sacrificed?
GILLES	I was merely joking, Sire.
CHARLES	You make too many jests. *(going to GILLES, kicking his foot)* Get off our throne!

> *GILLES bows and gets off the throne.*

CHARLES	Jehanne, here's a man for your army. The Great Pretender. The false king Bluebeard.

GILLES *(bowing)* Baron de Rais, at your service.

JEHANNE Noble Dauphin, why do you call this man Bluebeard?

CHARLES I've named him after his horse, of course.

The COURTIERS laugh.

GILLES They call me Bluebeard because I am bent over my writing so much, my beard gets caught in the ink.

JEHANNE What about your horse?

GILLES He's a good horse. I ride him frequently.

JEHANNE I don't understand.

GILLES The Dauphin was making a joke. When the Dauphin makes a joke, we laugh.

JEHANNE Why?

GILLES It's the way things are done here.

GEORGE is talking to CHARLES.

JEHANNE You can read and write?

GILLES *(loudly)* I have the largest library in all of France.

CHARLES *(calling back)* An exaggeration, Gilles.

GILLES Next to yours, of course, Sire.

CHARLES And George here. He has a large library.

GILLES His doesn't count, Sire. He doesn't read.

GEORGE I don't need to read, cousin. I have enough matter in my head.

GILLES Yes. It's very dense in there.

GEORGE	Showing off for the Maid, cousin? How odd. I didn't think you liked maids. Though this one appears to be your type.
GILLES	I find her very charming.
GEORGE	As charming as your wife?
GILLES	Yes.
GEORGE	As charming as your page?
GILLES	Cousin, I caught your jest the first time round. There's no need to labour the point. I prefer the company of men. That's no secret. I make a good soldier because of it. *(taking JEHANNE off to one side)* My wife and I meet once a year to produce children. It's a very Christian arrangement, though I don't suppose you know much about Christians.
JEHANNE	Pardon?
GILLES	*(conspiratorially)* The godmothers have asked me to keep watch over you.
JEHANNE	I don't think I understand you.
GILLES	The company? Does that bother you? No one is listening to our conversation. Secrets are always best discussed in crowds. We can step over here if you feel safer. *(guiding JEHANNE further over)*
JEHANNE	But I have no secrets.
GILLES	I was brought up in the old ways. I'm a bit of a hybrid. I see value in both religions. So, I'm both a good Christian and a witch.
JEHANNE	I am not a witch!
GILLES	Please, keep your voice down. It's the witches custom to dress in men's clothes.

JEHANNE	If I'm to lead the army, I should dress like a soldier.
GILLES	Women don't lead armies, as a rule.
JEHANNE	I don't care what women, as a rule, do.
GILLES	The least you can do is acknowledge the coven. I suppose it's only natural that you be cautious. Peasants are cautious by nature.
JEHANNE	I am not a peasant. My family doesn't have much money but my father is on the town council.
GILLES	You are cautious, though.
JEHANNE	I might be.
GILLES	I'm not. I wish I was. I put people off. I've put you off, haven't I?
JEHANNE	You're very bold.
GILLES	No bolder than you. I'll enjoy protecting you. I should warn you. They'll probably ask me to spy on you. To see if you're a witch.
JEHANNE	It's a little foolish of you, don't you think, to tell me that you might be spying on me.
GILLES	I find it hard to take the job seriously. It pays well, though. Most frivolous professions pay well.
JEHANNE	Who's paying you?
CHARLES	Gilles! You've monopolized the Maid long enough. The Archbishop's gone. Let's celebrate. *(announcing to the COURT)* JEHANNE THE MAID!

Scene Nine

GEORGE, GILLES DE RAIS, CHARLES, slumped in a chair.

ATTENDANT *(entering)* The Maid desires an audience with you, Sire.

CHARLES Tell her we're dying.

GILLES I don't think you want to alarm her, Sire.

CHARLES God no! You're right. She's exhausting enough, as it is. *(to ATTENDANT)* Tell her we're busy with affairs of state.

ATTENDANT leaves.

CHARLES *(to GEORGE and GILLES)* The King of Heaven has a lot of work for us. She's wearing us out and she's only been here for one month.

GEORGE Should we send her back, Sire?

CHARLES No, no, of course not. She's very charming. In small doses. We simply find it hard to keep up to her enthusiasms.

Act One / 61

GEORGE　　But of course. Our Dauphin is overburdened. Our Dauphin needs his energy to attend to important matters of state. *(to GILLES)* Why haven't you kept her occupied?

GILLES　　I've tried. I don't think she likes me much.

CHARLES　　It's all right, George. The Maid seems to only want to talk to us. We suppose it's only natural.

GEORGE　　Of course, Sire. Your native charisma.

CHARLES　　Oh really, George, really you musn't flatter us.

GEORGE　　Sire, it is not flattery. You are our beacon. You glow with Divine Wisdom.

CHARLES　　Oh really, George!

GEORGE　　The scintillation of your wit guides us all.

CHARLES　　No no, you mustn't. Really.

GEORGE　　You are our light at the end of the tunnel.

CHARLES　　*(disgusted)* That's enough, George. *(to GILLES)* Have you learned anything about her?

GILLES　　She seems virtuous enough. Do you think she is The One?

CHARLES　　You're asking me?!

GILLES　　Sorry, Sire.

CHARLES　　My Royal Blood grows thin. Sacrifices come in all shapes and all sizes. Remember that, Gilles.

GILLES　　Yes, Sire.

GEORGE　　*(to GILLES)* What about her Voices. Have you seen them?

GILLES　　I don't think you see voices, cousin.

GEORGE	Don't get smart with me. Informants. Have you noticed any?
GILLES	She appears to be genuine. She passed the examination at Poitiers.
GEORGE	I still think we should keep a close watch. That page we've given her is very stupid. We're not going to get anything out of him. He can't even remember names.
GILLES	I think he's rather sweet.
CHARLES	We say: Let us not look a gift horse in the mouth.
GEORGE	All right. We'll keep the page, but he's useless.
CHARLES	Not the page, George. The Maid. She may not be The One. Then again, she may be. Let's just send her off to Orleans and let her raise the siege before we die of exhaustion.
GEORGE	An excellent idea, Sire.
CHARLES	We are going to bed, now. *(getting up)*
GEORGE	Oh Sire, one more thing. Father Pasquerel is here to see you.
CHARLES	Who the hell is he?
GEORGE	You don't know him, Sire.
CHARLES	Well, what's he doing here, then?
GEORGE	I thought perhaps the Maid should have a...*(raising eyebrows)*...private confessor.
CHARLES	That's nice. We're going to bed. We need a nap.
GEORGE	Could you meet him, please, Sire. He's been waiting outside since this morning.

Act One / 63

CHARLES Oh God, can't someone else meet him. You know how we despise priests. Gilles, you be us. You meet him.

ATTENDANT *(announcing)* Father Pasquerel.

PRIEST comes in and kneels.

PRIEST Oh, Noble Dauphin.

CHARLES Oh, this really is too much! Everyone just barges in here at a moment's notice with complete disregard for our time! What is this! Open season at Chinon! Whose court is this, anyway!

GILLES The King of Heaven's?

CHARLES *(glaring at GILLES)* We are not amused. *(to PRIEST)* You! Get up!

The PRIEST gets up.

CHARLES What do you want?

PRIEST O most Magnificent Dauphin—

CHARLES Cut the slavering. George has hired you to be the Maid's private confessor. Is that it?

PRIEST Well-ah-well, ah...yes, Sire.

CHARLES How much?

PRIEST Oh-well-ah — One thousand francs for six months.

CHARLES Too much. Go away! *(turning to leave)*

GEORGE & PRIEST But, Sire!

PRIEST Sire, I could provide you with valuable information. I could tell you if the Maid is a witch.

GEORGE	Yes, Sire, he could.
CHARLES	Do you think she'd be dumb enough to let you know. Anyway, if she raises the siege, we don't care what she is. So, leave us.

GEORGE nods at the PRIEST.

PRIEST	I could — ah — I could reduce my price.
CHARLES	How much?
PRIEST	Eight hundred francs for five months
CHARLES	Too much. Five hundred francs for seven months. Take it or leave it.

The PRIEST looks upset.

CHARLES	I'm sure George could throw in a few hundred from his private kitty. You can report to him. And if it's really important, you can tell us. Now, we're going to bed. *(to GILLES)* De Rais!
GILLES	Sire?
CHARLES	You laugh out of the wrong side of your mouth.
GILLES	Sire?
CHARLES	We don't like it.
GILLES	I'll try not to do it again, Sire.

CHARLES leaves.

Scene Ten

JEHANNE in the forest.

JEHANNE Michael! Michael! Where are you! Come quickly. We don't have much time. They never leave me in peace. There's always someone around, yammering away. And when I finally steal some time alone, where are you! Michael!

COURTIER *(approaching)* Yes?

JEHANNE hides and the COURTIER looks around then leaves.

JEHANNE I don't like this job. I don't like these people. I'm tired of being sneered at and poked and prodded. I don't care if you don't come when I call you. I'm going back home.

MICHAEL *(appearing)* What's your hurry?

JEHANNE I knew that would bring you.

MICHAEL Tactics are unnecessary. I was here before.

JEHANNE Well, why didn't you come?

MICHAEL You seem to be in a bad mood. Why look for trouble.

JEHANNE	I'm leaving this place.
MICHAEL	Why?
JEHANNE	I've spent the last month passing tests. The Ladies of the Court had to check out my virginity. If it's still intact, it will be a miracle. Then I had to go to Poitiers and persuade the priests that I wasn't a witch. If one more person accuses me of being a witch, I shall scream.
MICHAEL	Maybe you are a witch.
JEHANNE	What!
MICHAEL	You have the power.
JEHANNE	Not enough. No one takes me seriously. They play tricks on me and then they laugh at me. A man today gave me armour that was too heavy, even by men's standards. Of course, I had to pretend that it was fine. I had to pretend I could ride and do battle exercises.
MICHAEL	You did it, didn't you?
JEHANNE	Yes, but—
MICHAEL	Be rude.
JEHANNE	Pardon?
MICHAEL	People will take you seriously if you're rude enough.
JEHANNE	Why?
MICHAEL	They confuse it with honesty.
JEHANNE	Honesty! Ha! There's not an honest man within miles of this place. And I'm no better. I lied to my parents. I should have told them about you. I should have at least sent them word so they'd know I'm all right.

Act One / 67

MICHAEL Jehanne the Maid, you are in a bad way. *(nodding)* Post partem depression.

JEHANNE Pardon?

MICHAEL Everything was aimed toward your meeting the Dauphin. You met him and now that it's over, you're depressed.

JEHANNE looks puzzled.

MICHAEL Sad.

JEHANNE He's not really worth all the hoopla, is he?

MICHAEL I wouldn't underestimate him. But, time for your next mission. Raise the siege at Orleans.

JEHANNE No.

MICHAEL What?

JEHANNE I don't need a pep talk. I need power. It's not enough to tell people what needs to be done. I have to be able to move them into action.

CATHERINE *(appearing)* You're losing your innocence, Jehanne the Maid.

JEHANNE *(seeing her)* Saint Catherine!

CATHERINE *(smiling)* It's fortunate that she knows who we are.

MARGARET *(entering, her features invisible)* Saves us having to make up a name.

MICHAEL Are you sure you want more power?

JEHANNE Yes.

CATHERINE You will live in your visions.

MARGARET	We will live our lives through you. Let us enter you.
JEHANNE	You won't take me over, will you?
MARGARET	Sometimes.
CATHERINE	Not always.
MARGARET	Open.
CATHERINE	Open.
JEHANNE	What if you're demons?
MARGARET	I will guard you against demons.
JEHANNE	Is that Saint Margaret?
MARGARET	Yes, Jehanne. I am Saint Margaret. Now Open!
VOICES	OPEN! *(they cluster around JEHANNE)*

>*MARGARET and MICHAEL withdraw. JEHANNE is in a trance state. CATHERINE is standing in front of JEHANNE. She is holding a sword. CATHERINE and JEHANNE are speaking together.*

JEHANNE & CATHERINE	We are Catherine, the Queen of Swords. We rule the air, the mind: thoughts, words, deeds. You are quite right, Jehanne.

>*JEHANNE stops speaking and, as her name is spoken, she comes out of her trance and listens to CATHERINE.*

Act One / 69

CATHERINE   What use are thoughts unless they are translated into deeds. But you must be careful of your thoughts lest they take on a form which you cannot control. Do not wish ill on anyone, Jehanne. It will come back to you, threefold. We are a lonely queen. That is the way it must be. We have a mission and we must fulfill it. You are in a nest of vipers. Seek friends where you can, but remember: you are a traveller through these parts and you will always be alone. Rely on your own native wit to guide you. Our sword will protect you. *(holding out sword)*

JEHANNE   *(bowing)* Thank you, Saint Catherine. *(reaching out to take sword)*

CATHERINE   *(withdrawing, still holding sword)* Buried in the ground behind the altar in Our Church at Fierbois. Five sacred crosses — Our Lady Mary and her consort Jesus engraved on the side. It is very rusty. They will have to clean it.

JEHANNE   I will go tomorrow.

CATHERINE   Jehanne, use your head. They want some proof from you. There is a man approaching. Use him.

GILLES   *(entering from behind, watching JEHANNE for a moment)* You spend a lot of time in the woods.

JEHANNE   *(without turning)* Yes.

GILLES   I didn't startle you just then?

JEHANNE   No. *(turning around to face him)* I knew you were there. There is a sword in the Church of Saint Catherine of Fierbois. It is the sword I shall use for battle.

GILLES   There wouldn't be a sword in a church, Jehanne. May I call you, Jehanne? We'll get the royal armourer to make you one.

JEHANNE	There is a sword in that church and I shall use it. It is buried in the ground behind the altar.
GILLES	Oh?
JEHANNE	It has five crosses on it and "Jesus Maria" written on the edge. It is very rusty and needs to be cleaned. That is the sword I must have. Will you please make sure that I get it.
GILLES	Well — ah — certainly. We'll send someone to go look for it. You're sure it's there? They're not going to like us digging in their church.
JEHANNE	I know it is there. I will go and dig it up myself.
GILLES	No, Jehanne. That won't be necessary. I'll take care of it. They're having a banquet in your honour. Shall we go?
JEHANNE	I'll be there presently.
GILLES	You know I've never seen you eat. Do you ever eat?
JEHANNE	Of course, I eat.
GILLES	Bread and milk and that's about it. There are wonderful things to eat in the world. Larks tongues glazed in honey, poached quail eggs, squab tarts, roast venison —
JEHANNE	You should hurry off to the banquet, then.
GILLES	If I were a peasant come to court, I would gorge myself senseless.
JEHANNE	I am not a—
GILLES	Sorry, I forgot. What I mean is, how long are you likely to be here? Charles has a very short attention span. The life of a favourite is one year — two years at the most.

JEHANNE   They're killed?

GILLES   You'll be replaced by someone else. Another luminary. But the idea is — once you've achieved the position, take advantage of it. You have no idea what you're involved in, have you?

JEHANNE   I know my part in it. I don't need to know any more.

GILLES   Once you get past the initial staggering boredom of it all, court politics can be rather amusing. Rule No. 1: Nobody likes Charles.

JEHANNE   I like him.

GILLES   No offense, but you're a nobody.

JEHANNE   Oh.

GILLES   A newcomer, then.

JEHANNE   Why doesn't anyone like the Dauphin?

GILLES   He's a creep.

JEHANNE   Are you sure?

GILLES   When you deal with creeps, particularly ones with power, being sure means being screwed. So far, he hasn't been a creep to me, but I'm staying out of his way. Then, there's George, my cousin. He's vicious. Charles is crazy about him.

JEHANNE   Don't say any more.

GILLES   They're not lovers. God no!

JEHANNE   Please stop. I don't want to know any more.

GILLES   Why not?

JEHANNE   It's not helping me.

GILLES You should know all you can. Knowledge is power.

JEHANNE No. It's not. You have knowledge. You can read and write. You've experienced far more than I have, but you have no power.

GILLES What nonsense! I have lots of power. I have thirteen castles in Brittany alone. I own half of France.

JEHANNE I am trying to unite France. Not keep track of her divisions. Besides which, you have property. That doesn't mean you have power.

GILLES It helps. If your Voices left you, you'd have no power.

JEHANNE How do you know about my Voices!

GILLES Charles told George and George told me.

JEHANNE Charles swore to me! He made a King's vow.

GILLES Like I said, he's a creep. Besides, he's not a king yet. He's very good at wriggling out of things on technicalities. Oh, by the way, they're going to send a priest after you.

JEHANNE Pardon?

GILLES I'm not doing a good enough job spying on you. You'll be having a Father Confessor following you about.

JEHANNE Oh.

GILLES Don't confess anything you don't want the whole world to know about. Save the juicy stuff for me. I'll appreciate it. Can't waste a good piece of flagellation on a priest. See you at supper. *(leaving)*

Scene Eleven

Chinon. CHARLES, GEORGE, JEHANNE and a FOOL and members of the court.

CHARLES   We love fools, don't you?

JEHANNE   I don't know what their purpose is.

CHARLES   Why, to make us laugh. *(clapping hand)* Fool, tell us a joke.

FOOL   Why is a civet cat like a privet hedge, Sire?

CHARLES   I don't know. Why, Fool?

FOOL   There's a strong odour that comes from both when the rutting season's on, Sire.

CHARLES   *(laughing)* Ho ho! Very good, Fool.

ALL in the room laugh.

CHARLES   Very funny.

JEHANNE   I don't get it.

FOOL   If the p's and c's are intertwined, they are the same creature.

CHARLES Ho ho! You are keen, Fool.

ALL in the room laugh.

JEHANNE I don't get it.

CHARLES Nobody understands the Fool's jokes. That's the beauty of it. If we laugh, they laugh. We like to see them laugh at jokes that aren't funny.

JEHANNE Sire, when are you going to let me raise the siege at Orleans?

CHARLES Oh God, not that again!

JEHANNE But Sire, I'm ready.

CHARLES Well, we're not. We need proof.

JEHANNE If you'd just let me go and do it, that should be proof enough.

GEORGE It costs a great deal of money to send troops to Orleans. Do you really think our Noble Dauphin should carry out a girl's whim.

JEHANNE It costs more to lose.

GEORGE Our Dauphin doesn't like to take foolish risks. You should consider yourself lucky to be here.

JEHANNE But I'm not doing anything.

GEORGE Then, perhaps we should send you back. Where's this sword we keep hearing about?

CHARLES *(glaring at him)* We?

GEORGE My most humblest apologies, Sire. *(to JEHANNE)* The sword I and the rest of the court keep hearing about. Where is it?

FOOL Why is a sword like a knave's belly?

Act One / 75

GEORGE Not now, Fool, please. *(to CHARLES)* He's off on his sword theme. Those are the only jokes he knows. *(to JEHANNE)* What about this sword.

JEHANNE Your cousin went off to get it for me.

GEORGE Gilles?! You sent him off to get your sword?! This is too much! He is a nobleman. He is no servant to a maid!

JEHANNE I didn't mean to offend him, Duke. I simply asked him to get my sword.

FOOL How likens the sword of Damocles to a gibbet?

JEHANNE He offered to go quite cheerfully.

FOOL The sword of Damocles hangs from a hair.

CHARLES *(yawning)* He must be as bored here as we are.

GEORGE I think you need a new Fool, Sire.

FOOL The gibbet hangs a—

CHARLES You're right. Fool! Dismissed!

FOOL But Sire, the gibbet.

CHARLES Ha ha! Very funny. *(motioning to crowd and they laugh)* Now go!

FOOL A coin, prithee, Sire.

CHARLES Oh God — there is no peace in this world. *(handing the FOOL a coin)*

FOOL That much, Sire?

CHARLES Don't be cheeky.

FOOL *(as he leaves)* Your generosity is like unto a dog's breakfast. It comes up when you least expect it.

CHARLES *(calling out to him)* You're fired! *(to JEHANNE)* Tell you what: if the sword is found and if it's as you say it is, five crosses, all that rigmarole, then we will send you and our best men to Orleans within the week.

JEHANNE Why not the next day, Sire.

CHARLES Oh. Not next week? Well, I suppose we could exert ourselves. All right. The next day, then.

JEHANNE Promise, Sire?

CHARLES Our King's vow.

JEHANNE Perhaps, Sire, if it's not too much trouble, you could please make a Dauphin's vow as well.

CHARLES Very well. Dauphin's vow then. We find your single-mindedness somewhat disturbing. You're not exactly stimulating company. You don't eat. You don't carouse.

JEHANNE I'm not very good at carousing, Sire.

CHARLES You could at least try.

ATTENDANT Baron Gilles de Rais.

GILLES *(entering carrying sword, then bowing)* Noble Dauphin. *(bowing to JEHANNE)* Gentle Maid. *(raising sword above head)* The sword of Saint Catherine.

The crowd gasps.

GILLES Found under the altar of her church at Fierbois. *(displaying sword)* Five crosses etched on the blade.

The crowd gasps again.

Act One / 77

GILLES	"Jesus - Maria" engraved on the edge. This is the sword of the Maid's prophecy. I offer it to her with my fond allegiance to be at her side always in battle.
CHARLES	Oh, this is very ceremonial. Jehanne, you must go receive the sword from the Baron.
JEHANNE	*(taking GILLE's hand)* I take your hand that we will always be together in battle. And I take Catherine's sword that we will share victory for France!

> *JEHANNE and GILLES raise sword above heads. GILLES looks at JEHANNE. JEHANNE looks at GILLES and bursts out laughing.*

GILLES	*(still keeping sword above his head)* Don't lose your concentration.
JEHANNE	I'm sorry, sire.
GILLES	This is a pivotal moment. This is the moment when the bond was forged between us.
JEHANNE	*(starting to snicker)* She never liked you, sire.
GILLES	*(dropping arm)* What do you know about it! You weren't even there!
JEHANNE	I can feel it.
CHARLES	Oh, don't get mystical on us!
GEORGE	*(to GILLES)* Why do you put up with that kid? He ruins our performance every time!
GILLES	*(to audience)* This is François. François has been paid a large sum of money to keep his mouth shut and only open it to say his lines. François has been hired because he is the spitting image of Jehanne the Maid. I thought you might like to know what she really looked like.

JEHANNE	*(tapping breasts)* Fake.
GILLES	That is the only reason he has been hired. As an actor, he is execrable.
JEHANNE	No, I'm not, sire. I'm good. I really get into my role.
GEORGE	Yes, but then you come out of it and talk about it.
JEHANNE	I played Jehanne all right when we did the play at Orleans.
GILLES	Playing it twice does not necessarily mean that you are good. I looked high and low for the perfect double for Jehanne and unfortunately, François, you were the only one I could find.
GEORGE	He was looking low at the time.
JEHANNE	You only looked at boys.
GILLES	You think I'd cast a girl in this role?! The role needs Strength. Purity.
JEHANNE	And you think I have that, sire?
GILLES	No, but I had to take what I could get. So, I settled for looks.

The PRIEST enters.

CHARLES	Oh God, it's Gilles' bête-noir.

CHARLES and GEORGE leave hurriedly. JEHANNE follows them.

PRIEST	I don't seem to be very popular around here.

GILLES is distracted.

PRIEST	Why don't they like me?
GILLES	Pay no attention. Actors are a scurvy lot.

Act One / 79

PRIEST   Oh. *(pause)* Marshall, Jean Le Ferron is here to speak with you.

GILLES   Who's he?

PRIEST   He's a priest. Acting for the Bishop of Nantes. About your castles.

GILLES   My castles?

PRIEST   You sold three cstles to him — Prigny, Vüe, Bois-aux-Tre'aux. And the parish of St. Michel.

GILLES   Oh yes. Amazing what you do when you're drunk and need money. Tell him I've changed my mind. I'm reclaiming those properties.

PRIEST   Then you better return the money.

GILLES   Too late. It's spent. *(gesturing to stage)*

PRIEST   You are totally irresponsible! Why are you doing this play again! Haven't you lost enough!

GILLES   You think it's just a play, do you. *(laughing)* Ah Pierre, how little you know me.

PRIEST   *(pacing)* I can't look after you, anymore. I simply can't do it.

GILLES   You're sweet. *(kissing PRIEST on the cheek)*

PRIEST   And none of that! Do you hear me!

GILLES   Yes, Pierre.

PRIEST   Your weakness of the flesh—

GILLES   Our weakness. You share it.

PRIEST I share your taste. Not your appetite. Moderation is the keynote. Besides, I took a vow of celibacy. Not chastity. It's not my problem if people confuse the two. I'll talk to Le Ferron. I'll see if I can put him off. But you shouldn't antagonize the Bishop.

GILLES He's a greedy fool.

PRIEST That doesn't make him any less powerful.

GILLES He can't touch me. *(starting to leave)*

PRIEST Also — there's a woman outside. Her daughter's gone missing and she was last seen at the gates.

GILLES Surely, you don't expect me to talk to her.

PRIEST Someone should.

GILLES You do it, then.

PRIEST No!

GILLES *(pulling out money)* She'll need the comfort of the Church.

PRIEST *(taking money)* Oh, all right. But just this once. *(exiting)*

PRIEST exits. GILLES leaves in opposite direction. ISABELLE enters.

Act One / 81

Scene Twelve

ISABELLE, alone on stage

ISABELLE Jeanette, why did you run away? Your uncle didn't know you were going to do such a thing. He's been apologizing to us ever since. What can you do with a mad daughter. What if the Dauphin rejects you? What will you do, then? Don't you know that every virgin in France wants to be the Chosen One. Anything could happen. You could become a whore. Or worse yet, the Christians could get hold of you and make you into a nun. You have the temperament for it. So secretive. Who knows what goes on in the minds of our children? Please come home, Jeanette. Whore, nun, whatever you become, don't be too proud to come home.

End of Act One.

Act Two, Scene One

GILLES *(entering)* Why do children leave home? What lures them away? I don't lure them. They come to me. In droves. I used to think it was because they were poor and I was rich. But you people live in comparative luxury and your children still run away. Is the present always so bleak that people are willing to sacrifice what they have for the promise of a better future? François?

JEHANNE Yeah?

GILLES Why did you come to me?

JEHANNE shrugs.

GILLES I'm serious. Why did you run away from home?

JEHANNE I was bored.

GILLES Why?

JEHANNE There was nothing to do. Well, actually, there was lots to do. But it was always the same. Feed the chickens, dig up the fields, fetch water. The same arguments. I could see that nothing was going to change. It was going to be like that for the rest of my life. So I left.

GILLES Why do you stay here? I'm not very nice to you.

JEHANNE	It's true, sire. You're not. But I'm too tired to leave.
GILLES	Did you always want to leave?
JEHANNE	No. At first, I thought I was in Paradise. You gave me all these beautiful clothes — all these great things to eat. I'd never eaten so much in my life. And you said such nice things to me. I thought I was really special. I didn't know about the others. When I found out about them, I saw it was just a game you were playing. Only, I happened to look like her so I got to stick around.
GILLES	I think we should resume the play.
JEHANNE	You don't care what I think! You never listen to me! You just want me here so you can pretend I'm someone else!
GILLES	François, I think you are the sort of person who will always be dissatisfied with your lot in life. Whatever you have, it will never be enough.
JEHANNE	I want a new costume. I'm tired of wearing this.
	GILLES leaves and returns with white armour, and gives it to JEHANNE
GILLES	Here. Jehanne's armour. We are now in Orleans. Jehanne is going to raise the siege. You remember the play we did before?
JEHANNE	Of course I remember. I was in it.
GILLES	Not for the entire run, François. There was a boy before you .
JEHANNE	Oh. Did he look like Jehanne, too?
GILLES	No. He was just a beautiful boy. *(stroking Jehanne's cheek)* You bear an uncanny resemblance to her.

Act Two / 85

JEHANNE	What happened to him?
GILLES	I found you, François.
JEHANNE	Yes, but what happened to him?
GILLES	Why the sudden concern? You couldn't have cared less at the time. You knew you were replacing him. That was all that mattered to you.
JEHANNE	*(looking at costume)* Oh Jesus! *(throwing armour down)* Why does every costume I wear have tits! It's not fair, sire! Everyone else can wear their costumes again. I can't wear mine. I'm going to look pretty stupid feeding the chickens in a white armour with tits!
GILLES	You haven't fed chickens for two years, François.
JEHANNE	It's the principle of the thing.
GILLES	You don't have any principles, either, François.
JEHANNE	Why do you say these mean things to me? It's like you're trying to make me into something.
GILLES	I have made you into something. You were a starving illiterate peasant when I found you. I've fed you, clothed you, housed you. I've given you the appearance of a young nobleman. You should be grateful.
JEHANNE	I am not your slave.
GILLES	You prefer to be called servant. Very well, but the fact remains: you have been bought. I am your master and you shall do as I say. *(pointing to floor)* Now, lie down!
JEHANNE	You're not going to...?
GILLES	Lie Down!

Lights start to come down.

JEHANNE lies down. GILLES leaves.
CATHERINE and MARGARET enter.

CATHERINE *(whispering)* Blood.

MARGARET *(whispering)* Blood.

CATHERINE Jehanne. Blood.

MARGARET Frenchmen are losing blood.

CATHERINE & MARGARET JEHANNE!

JEHANNE *(sitting up with a start)* Hah!

MARGARET French blood.

CATHERINE The Southern Gate.

JEHANNE *(starting to strap on armour)* What?! Why didn't anyone tell me?!

CATHERINE Mascot.

MARGARET *(derisively)* Mascot!

CATHERINE and MARGARET exit.

JEHANNE *(calling out while strapping armour on)* MINGUET! WHERE ARE YOU! HELP ME WITH THIS!

JEHANNE searches about for sword and standard, grabs them, rushes out the door, bumps into GILLES, accompanied by young boy, played by Michael.

JEHANNE *(to boy, loudly)* MINGUET! WHERE HAVE YOU BEEN! FRENCHMEN ARE DYING AS WE SPEAK! WHY DIDN'T YOU WAKE ME! *(cuffing him)*

MICHAEL Ow! *(rubbing ear)* The men told me not to.

JEHANNE	From now on you do what I tell you! Where were you, anyway?
MICHAEL	Um — ah — um...
JEHANNE	*(to GILLES)* Where's my horse?
GILLES	You're asking me?!
JEHANNE	What are you doing with my page?
GILLES	We were coming to give you the news
JEHANNE	If you expect me to believe that crock, you've got another thought coming. I can't waste time talking to fops. I'm going to fight with the men. *(starting to leave, then calling out)* SOUND THE ALARM! QUICK! THE SOUTHERN GATE IS UNDER ATTACK!
GILLES	Call me a fop, will you. I'm a better soldier than any of them.
JEHANNE	Prove it! *(exiting)*

Scene Two

          JEHANNE, alone.

ENGLISH SOLDIER   *(approaching with sword, smiling menacingly)* Well, if it isn't the French whore.

JEHANNE   I am Jehanne the Maid. Don't come any closer or you will pay for it.

SOLDIER   I plan to collect. *(advancing on her)*

JEHANNE   *(drawing sword)* Saint Catherine, protect me!

          They have a sword fight.

JEHANNE   I don't want to hurt you. You'd better go. I'm not allowed to shed blood.

SOLDIER   Oh really, you don't say? I like to shed blood. Particularly, virgin blood. How'd you like eight inches of pink ramrod up your cannon!

          JEHANNE is momentarily stunned by the remark. The SOLDIER forces JEHANNE to drop sword. He grabs her. GILLES enters, stabs the SOLDIER in the back. CATHERINE enters and smiles at JEHANNE.

JEHANNE   *(falling on knees)* Thank you, Saint Catherine.

Act Two / 89

GILLES What are you thanking her for? I'm the one who saved your life.

JEHANNE She sent you to me.

GILLES I could have sworn I came by myself.

CATHERINE Use him.

JEHANNE Use him?

GILLES For what? Compost? *(looking at dead man)* Normally, I never kill a man when his back is turned. It seems unfair, somehow. What the hell were you doing here?!

CATHERINE He will serve us. Plant the idea in his mind. He will do the rest. *(exiting)*

JEHANNE *(to GILLES)* I forbid you to swear in my presence.

GILLES You were almost killed just now, but really, you don't need to thank me.

JEHANNE It was not my time to die.

GILLES It looked like it to me. If you weren't killed, you would have lost your virginity in pretty short order. You shouldn't join in our battles.

JEHANNE Don't tell me what I should or shouldn't do.

GILLES Then you should at least have the sense to know where to fight. No one. Not even the bravest captain fights hand-to-hand in English territory. That's not courageous. That's simply stupid. Where are your troops? They're way back there. Fighting in sensible places. And where are the captains? They're even further behind, ordering everyone else on ahead. If you're going to be a soldier, be a captain. You'll live longer.

JEHANNE I'm as good a soldier as the rest of you.

GILLES Your sword play's not bad. Though you shouldn't tell the enemy that you're not allowed to kill him. It only encourages him.

JEHANNE I told him he would die if he fought me. And he died, didn't he?

GILLES Your logic is impeccable.

JEHANNE I can think just as well as the rest of you. And I am not a mascot!

GILLES "Impeccable" is not an insult.

JEHANNE Oh.

GILLES And I am not a fop. *(pause)* You know, we make a good team. Do you like working with me?

JEHANNE Yes, except for one thing.

GILLES What?

JEHANNE You are working with me. *(exiting)*

GILLES *(bellowing)* GOD HELP THE FIRST CHRISTIAN! *(smiling)* My war cry. *(following JEHANNE)*

Scene Three

War council. GILLES DE RAIS, GEORGE, THE BASTARD OF ORLEANS and LA HIRE. THE BASTARD and LA HIRE are played by MICHAEL and CATHERINE.

JEHANNE *(outside)* BASTARD! BASTARD! ARE YOU IN THERE!

GEORGE Oh Jesus, who told her to come! *(to GILLES)* Did you tell her?

JEHANNE BASTARD!

BASTARD I wish she wouldn't call me that. *(opening door)*

JEHANNE *(rushing in)* What is this? A council? Are you having a war council without me?

BASTARD Well, not exactly, Jehanne.

JEHANNE Don't lie to me, Bastard. How can I help you if you don't let me in on your plans?

GEORGE Because when we tell you our plans, you tell us they're all wrong.

JEHANNE They are all wrong.

GEORGE There! She's doing it again!

JEHANNE	If we do what the King of Heaven advises, we will win. It's as simple as that.
BASTARD	Still, we have to plan. The King of Heaven hasn't been very specific.
JEHANNE	We took the Southern gate, didn't we.
GEORGE	We could just as easily have lost our skins on that one.
JEHANNE	I didn't see your skin out there fighting.
GEORGE	The King of Heaven didn't tell me where to go.
JEHANNE	You have been with your council and I have been with mine. Believe me, my council will hold good and will be accomplished and yours will come to naught. *(starting to leave)*
BASTARD	Wait! You have a plan?
JEHANNE	The King of Heaven has given me one. Yes.
BASTARD	What is it?
JEHANNE	Are you asking out of idle curiosity or because you intend to take the advice?

The MEN look at one another.

JEHANNE	Do as you please. I don't want to fight in an army that loses. Let me know when you decide to win and I'll help you.
BASTARD	Please, Jehanne, what is your plan?
JEHANNE	We will go after the main fortress.
GEORGE	That's ridiculous!
BASTARD	Jehanne, how exactly are we supposed to take the fort?

Act Two / 93

JEHANNE Very simple. We get all our men together and we attack.

GEORGE You call that a strategy?!

JEHANNE The English won't be expecting it.

GEORGE You can say that again.

JEHANNE We should give the English one last chance to retreat. I shall send a letter.

GEORGE Not another bloody letter!

JEHANNE *(glaring at him)* I cannot shed innocent blood. They should be warned. And La Hire!

LA HIRE *(starting up)* Uh!

JEHANNE La Hire, how can we expect the men to follow us if we don't set a good example.

LA HIRE I haven't sworn in two days, Jehanne.

JEHANNE I'm talking about your whore.

LA HIRE My woman?

JEHANNE Your whore.

LA HIRE I can't ask Madeline to leave. She's been with me for three years. She'll be damna— very hurt.

JEHANNE Stop paying her and you'll find she leaves of her own accord. *(to MEN)* That goes for all of you! *(exiting)*

GEORGE Why that little witch! I'd like to wring her neck. *(to BASTARD)* How could you let her take over like that!

BASTARD Because for the first time in years, we're winning. We win when we follow her and we lose when we don't.

GEORGE But our council! She just barges right in—

BASTARD The more I see of the Maid, the more I realize that councils are pure affectation. Busy work for losers. *(to GILLES)* Oh, by the way, Baron, good work today! *(clapping him on the back)* You're coming along.

GILLES Thank you.

LA HIRE Maybe if she dressed like a soldier.

BASTARD She already is dressed like a soldier.

LA HIRE Not the Maid. Madeleine! Yeah, that would work.

BASTARD and LA HIRE leave.

GEORGE I suppose you think I should congratulate you on your escapade at the Southern Gate this morning.

GILLES It wasn't an escapade, cousin. It was a victory. The Maid and I work well together.

GEORGE Don't encourage her, Gilles. What was she doing there, anyway? Why doesn't she just stay in her room and talk to God? Why does she have to go out and talk to Him on our battlefields!

GILLES The King of Heaven.

GEORGE Whatever. God. King of Heaven. Same thing.

GILLES Not necessarily.

GEORGE What do you mean?

GILLES Forget it.

GEORGE The King of Heaven is a code word for the Devil? Is that it?

GILLES I'm sorry. Forget that I mentioned it.

GEORGE	*(paying him)* Thank you, Gilles. I never realized the discrepancy before.
GILLES	Please. I didn't mean it that way.
GEORGE	Don't fool yourself. That girl is a witch. I thought you'd be immune to her charms but you're doing her bidding just like everyone else.
GILLES	She has no power over me.
GEORGE	Already, you've protected her. You find her attractive, don't you?
GILLES	What does that have to do with it?
GEORGE	All spells begin with attraction.
GILLES	In that case, the attraction is mutual.
GEORGE	I think not. I've watched her with you. She's using you. She may look and act like a boy, but she's not.
GILLES	I wasn't always interested in boys, George.
GEORGE	You don't say. Well then, how is your wife?
GILLES	Does my wife have to represent all womanhood. As it happens, she's pregnant. Do I pass your test?
GEORGE	It's a start. Who's the father?
GILLES	You flatter me.
GEORGE	A tactless remark. I couldn't resist it. Congratulations! *(leaving)* Beware the Maid, Gilles. If you allow her, she will consume you.
GILLES	I didn't know you were so concerned for me, cousin.
GEORGE	Blood is thicker than water. Remember whose side you're on. *(exiting)*

Scene Four

> *JEHANNE, CATHERINE, and MARGARET. CATHERINE and MARGARET are on opposite sides of the stage. MARGARET's face is obscured. JEHANNE enters. CATHERINE accosts her.*

CATHERINE Why did you drive the whores out of the camp!

JEHANNE They were corrupting the men.

CATHERINE That is not why you had them removed. Don't lie to me.

JEHANNE I don't like them.

MARGARET You have no business sending them away.

JEHANNE Yes. I do. It's my army.

CATHERINE It's our army. The whores are your own kind.

JEHANNE I have nothing in common with those women.

MARGARET Pride, Jehanne.

CATHERINE Are you afraid of what you might have become?

Act Two / 97

JEHANNE	No. I'd never be like that. Never! Stop telling me what to do all the time.
CATHERINE	You want our advice.
JEHANNE	You never leave me alone. I can't think.
CATHERINE	You're not supposed to think. We do that for you.
JEHANNE	Maybe, I'd like to think for myself for a change. I'm not stupid.
MARGARET	Pride, Jehanne.

GILLES enters, watches JEHANNE.

JEHANNE	Stop saying that!
CATHERINE	She's warning you. Don't abuse the power. You are obstinate, Jehanne the Maid.
MARGARET	Your man is here.
JEHANNE	*(not turning around)* I don't like it when you spy on me, Gilles.
GILLES	Are you talking to them now?
JEHANNE	*(turning and facing him)* Don't spy on me!
GILLES	Where do you get your power?
CATHERINE	Ooooh — he wants it.
MARGARET	He's begging for it.
GILLES	How do you get people to do what you want?
JEHANNE	I don't understand.
GILLES	You tell them something and they do it. They obey you.

JEHANNE	They don't obey me. They obey the King of Heaven.
MARGARET	Very good, Jehanne. You have learned your lesson well.
GILLES	It must be nice to have all these people fawning over you.
MARGARET	He'll do.
CATHERINE	There are limits to your power, Jehanne. You must ground yourself through that man. He will carry on the other tasks.
GILLES	Are you listening to me?
JEHANNE	Yes, Gilles.
CATHERINE	He wants your power. Share it with him.
MARGARET	Seduce him.
JEHANNE	What!
GILLES	Are you all right? You look faint.
CATHERINE	The intention is what counts. A kiss.
MARGARET	A kiss.

CATHERINE and MARGARET leave.

JEHANNE	Do you find me attractive, Gilles?
GILLES	Oh — well — I'm not attracted to women, as a rule. But then, I don't think of you as a woman. You're a girl, aren't you?
JEHANNE	You prefer boys, don't you, Gilles. My page, Minguet, did he please you?
GILLES	Oh — ah —

JEHANNE	You're flustered.
GILLES	Ah — ah, no. I'm not.
JEHANNE	Why do you dislike women so?
GILLES	I don't dislike them. I'm not sexually attracted to them. Why is that a crime?
JEHANNE	I never said it was.
GILLES	These days, sex itself is a crime. You wouldn't have got too far if you hadn't been a virgin. That's what I can't understand. Witches use sex to bind their spells. How can you be a virgin witch?
JEHANNE	There are ways of having sex and still being a virgin. You should know that, Gilles.
GILLES	WHAT?
JEHANNE	And when it comes to spells, a kiss will do.
GILLES	Ah — ah — are you saying you're a witch?
JEHANNE	You want some of my power, don't you, Gilles?
GILLES	Well — ah—
JEHANNE	Would you like me to share it with you?

JEHANNE approaches GILLES.

GILLES	Oh — ah— *(nodding)*
JEHANNE	Gilles, you're trembling. You must not misuse it. You're sure you'd like it?

GILLES nods vigorously.

JEHANNE	The power is to serve.

JEHANNE kisses him. The kiss lasts a long time. JEHANNE/FRANÇOIS pulls away.

JEHANNE   You never kiss me like that.

GILLES   Yes, I did. Just now.

JEHANNE   That was her you were kissing. That wasn't me.

GILLES   Have it your way. *(starting to leave)*

JEHANNE   Why didn't you save her?

GILLES   There was nothing I could do.

JEHANNE   Did you see her get burned?

GILLES   *(stopping)* No.

JEHANNE   Are you sure she was burned? People say—

GILLES   Yes, François. She was burned.

JEHANNE   It must have been a horrible death.

GILLES   Yes.

JEHANNE   You're not planning to include that scene, are you?

GILLES   Oh, for God's sake, François. I've told you time and time again. This is a victory play. This play celebrates Jehanne's victory at the Siege of Orleans.

JEHANNE   Well — God said that you were going to burn me at the stake.

GILLES   God? God spoke to you?!

JEHANNE   No. Not God. "God!" That horrible old faggot. I don't know his name. He said you were going to burn me at the stake.

Act Two / 101

GILLES He's just teasing you.

JEHANNE He was building up a huge pile of kindling as he said it.

GILLES You will never suffer a martyr's death, François.

GILLES makes a signal. GEORGE appears. They confer.

JEHANNE I don't understand you, Sire.

GILLES No. And you never will. *(exiting with GEORGE)*

CATHERINE enters. She is carrying an arrow. She smiles at JEHANNE. JEHANNE smiles back. CATHERINE lunges forward, tries to stab JEHANNE with the arrow. JEHANNE gasps and leaps back.

CATHERINE Are you prepared to die! *(lunging at her again)*

JEHANNE *(dodging her)* NO!

CATHERINE You must not be afraid to face your fate.

JEHANNE I'm not going to die, though, am I? I still have a lot of work to do.

CATHERINE You are going to be wounded in battle, tomorrow. Blood will flow from above your breast. It is necessary.

JEHANNE Why?

CATHERINE Are you afraid?

JEHANNE Yes. Why is it necessary?

CATHERINE You are working magic. You must pay in some way. You will take Orleans tomorrow.

JEHANNE	Yes.
CATHERINE	You have not told the man what we look like, have you?
JEHANNE	No.
CATHERINE	*(pointing arrow at JEHANNE's breast)* Have you?
JEHANNE	No. Catherine, you're frightening me.
CATHERINE	Power is a double-edged sword.
	MARGARET enters. Her face is not visible.
MARGARET	You still have not restored the whores to the camp.
JEHANNE	The men would think it strange if I changed my orders.
MARGARET	You're not going to obey us?
JEHANNE	No. I hate those women!
MARGARET	Don't lash out at your fears or they will conquer you. You should face them.
JEHANNE	But I don't see why—
CATHERINE	You will be wounded in battle, tomorrow. Face that! *(plunging arrow in JEHANNE's breast)*
	JEHANNE staggers backward. MARGARET and CATHERINE withdraw. GILLES and the PRIEST enter. GILLES catches hold of JEHANNE.
PRIEST	Oh Lord, it is just as she predicted. A wound above the breast. It is just as she said! A prophecy! *(crossing himself)*

Act Two / 103

GILLES You don't have to be so bloody cheerful about it. Be still, Jehanne. I am going to pull the arrow out.

JEHANNE No. I'll do it myself.

GILLES *(to PRIEST)* Quick! A cloth!

PRIEST I don't have one on me. I'll have to go back—

> *GILLES rips cloth off PRIEST's surplice.*

PRIEST Hey! Wait just a—

> *JEHANNE pulls arrow out. GILLES staunches the blood.*

PRIEST Oooooh. Blood makes me queasy.

GILLES Let me put some ointment on it. *(pulling a vial out of his pocket)*

PRIEST What sort of ointment?

GILLES A balm for wounds.

PRIEST *(grabbing it, sniffing it)* It smells of herbs. It's witches ointment. This is sorcery!

GILLES Listen, you meddling old fart! Do you want her to die!

JEHANNE Don't worry, Gilles. I won't die. A dressing of olive oil and lard will do.

GILLES We should retreat. We've been at it all day and getting nowhere. I'll ask the Bastard to sound the trumpets.

JEHANNE No! Give me some time alone. In the grove. I shall find out what we have to do. *(exiting)*

PRIEST *(to GILLES)* Why did you rip my surplice?

GILLES   I needed some cloth.

PRIEST   That is very expensive material.

GILLES   So, I'll buy you another.

PRIEST   With what? The straw in your basement?

GILLES   I've explained this to you before, Pierre. Everything is made up of particles. And each particle has a centre. And each centre contains the essence of energy. So, if I split that centre, the energy is released. And I can use it to do what I want.

PRIEST   It's still not going to change the straw into gold.

GILLES   It could, though. If the particles split and rearranged themselves, they could be transformed into anything.

PRIEST   Yes, like yellow dust.

GILLES   You interrupted me. I couldn't finish the invocation.

PRIEST   Oh — sorry — it's all my fault, then. Just don't rip my surplice, eh. Anyway, alchemy's a heresy.

GILLES   Is that the latest edict from the Bishop of Nantes? He's being very creative with the dogma. Has he figured out a way to confiscate my property, yet?

PRIEST   Yes, as a matter of fact—

GILLES   Later. I don't want to talk about Commerce. We're making Art. We're paying tribute to Jehanne.

PRIEST   If you'd paid her ransom, she'd still be alive. And you wouldn't have needed a tribute.

GILLES   You think it was as simple as that.

Act Two / 105

PRIEST   I know it was. It's done all the time. The English bought Talbot back, didn't they? They were waiting for Charles to make an offer.

GILLES   The King had no money.

PRIEST   Yes, but you did.

GILLES   We all have to die, sometime, Pierre, Can you really see Jehanne as some plump matron, whiling out her days in Domremy, milking cows and worrying about her children?

PRIEST   So, she should be burned because the image of her alive doesn't appeal to your aesthetic sense.

GILLES   Her mission, Pierre. That's what she lived for. This sacred virginity of hers that she guarded so ferociously. Men died because they dared to insult it. Was she simply to go back to Domremy and just give it away to some hapless boob of a husband. Don't you see, her mission would have come to naught. She would have been another court favourite with mystical leanings. Nothing more. We would have won a few battles, but the war would have gone on. The power, to be any use at all, had to be consummated.

PRIEST   At least, it's not on my conscience.

GILLES   It should be. It was your Church that brought her to trial.

PRIEST   Poor simple innocent.

GILLES   Don't be naive, Pierre. She was a monster.

PRIEST   Pardon?

GILLES   Ruthless. She won't like my version of events. But I've tried being polite.

PRIEST   Polite?

GILLES	My Mystery play. That was polite. We ended it at Orleans. When she was in her glory. Before the worm started to turn. But it didn't summon her. Too many lies. Too much flattery. Perhaps that's why she didn't come. Who can say what the spirits desire.
PRIEST	You're trying to raise Jehanne's ghost?!
GILLES	Ssssh.
PRIEST	But that's sorcery!
GILLES	An invocation. Harmless.
PRIEST	Sorcery! Then it's true!
GILLES	What? What are you getting in such a snit about?
PRIEST	Jean Le Ferron was inspecting the Chateau Tiffauges for the Bishop.
GILLES	Oh God! Him again!
PRIEST	He found the bones of a small child and a bloody cloth in the basement. He was appalled and disgusted.
GILLES	Serves him right for trespassing. *(starting to leave)*
PRIEST	*(grabbing him)* What do you do in your castles? Where do the boys go!
GILLES	Now that you mention it, Pierre. I do need some more.
PRIEST	What do you do with the ones I send you?
GILLES	Are you trying to weasel out of our agreement?
PRIEST	I will not be dragged down with you! Look, give the Bishop your lands. That should appease him. He might overlook the other things.

GILLES	You believe that cock and bull story!
PRIEST	Just give them the land.
GILLES	They'll get my land over my dead body!
PRIEST	That is a distinct possibility.
GILLES	Are you threatening me! *(pulling out a knife)*
PRIEST	*(backing off)* A warning. No more. *(leaving)*

GILLES leaves in the other direction.

Scene Five

           JEHANNE in a grove. CATHERINE *and* MARGARET *are with her.*

CATHERINE   You must rally the men.

JEHANNE   I'm so tired. Maybe we should begin again tomorrow.

CATHERINE   The time is ripe. Now or never!

MARGARET   Now or never!

           CATHERINE and MARGARET repeat "Now or Never!" in an echoing effect.

JEHANNE   Please! Speak softly. My head aches with your voices.

CATHERINE   Have courage, Jehanne. You will gain strength from your wound. Put your hand on it.

           JEHANNE puts hand on her breast.

CATHERINE   The blood that flows above your breast will give you power.

MARGARET   You must not waste it. You must use it tonight.

CATHERINE   We feel very strong. Guard your power. Don't let the men take it from you.

GILLES enters. CATHERINE and MARGARET leave.

GILLES Jehanne.

JEHANNE I said I wanted to be alone, Gilles.

GILLES I was just checking to see if you were all right. *(taking her hand)*

JEHANNE *(removing hand)* I'll be fine. Now please, leave me.

GILLES You're very cold. Are you always so unpleasant when someone saves your life?

JEHANNE There's an old saying from my parts. If you save someone's life, then you are bound to that person for the rest of your life.

GILLES A spiritual marriage of sorts?

JEHANNE No. It's much simpler than that. You are now my servant.

GILLES The hell I am!

JEHANNE Don't swear, Gilles. Then we're agreed. You didn't save my life.

GILLES Jehanne?

JEHANNE Yes.

GILLES Would you kiss me again?

JEHANNE Why?

GILLES I liked it when you kissed me. *(going to kiss her)*

JEHANNE *(steps back, laughing, clutching heart)* Oh! I shouldn't laugh. It hurts.

GILLES Is the idea so ludicrous to you?

JEHANNE   I shared my power with you, Gilles. That is all.

GILLES   But nothing happened. I don't have any power. Nobody does what I tell them anymore than they used to.

JEHANNE   So — it's my power you're after. Not my kisses.

GILLES   I want both.

JEHANNE   Oh yes, the hybrid. You want to be a witch and a Christian. You want my love and my power. You're greedy, Gilles.

GILLES   The old ways are dying. We should merge the two religions. You and your old ways must adapt to the times.

JEHANNE   You keep accusing me of belonging to the Old Religion. I believe in my Voices.

GILLES   And where are they from?

JEHANNE   Heaven, of course.

GILLES   You're sure about that?

JEHANNE   Yes, I'm sure. They're not evil. They've never asked me to do anything evil.

GILLES   No. You do it by proxy. I do the killing for you.

JEHANNE   You make an excellent proxy.

GILLES   Maybe I don't want to do your dirty work. I've seen the blood rush to your cheeks every time we go to battle. It's eerie. You seem to feed off it. Is that where you get your power? Do you bind your spells with our blood?

JEHANNE   I tried to share my power with you, Gilles, but it didn't take hold.

GILLES   It took hold all right. You know full well it did!

Trumpet sounds.

JEHANNE They're sounding the retreat. They can't retreat! You were supposed to tell them not to! Where's my standard?!

GILLES I don't know. How should I know where your standard is!

JEHANNE runs out.

GILLES I've got better things to do than chase after Maids and their lost standards.

JEHANNE *(offstage)* GILLES!

GILLES runs after her.

Scene Six

> *The French court. CHARLES, GEORGE and JEHANNE. MICHAEL is present as a courtier. CATHERINE and MARGARET are ladies of the court.*

CHARLES You've done a splendid job, Jehanne. Hasn't she done a splendid job, George!

GEORGE *(without enthusiasm)* Yes, splendid.

CHARLES We never expected you to capture Orleans in a week.

JEHANNE That was the allotted time you gave me, Sire. And now, we must go to Rheims.

CHARLES Rheims? Why?

JEHANNE For your coronation, noble Dauphin.

CHARLES Yes. Well. All in good time.

JEHANNE I don't have that much time, Sire. It must be this week.

CHARLES We don't have anything to wear.

JEHANNE But surely, Sire—

CHARLES Coronations are very expensive, aren't they, George.

Act Two / 113

GEORGE	Yes. They are.
CHARLES	Proper robes for us and our entourage. Music, food for the entire town. And a crown. We don't know where the crown has disappeared to. It will exhaust our funds.
JEHANNE	But Dauphin, isn't there an official coronation robe?
CHARLES	Oh — that old thing. It's quite filthy. It will need to be cleaned. We're too short for it. It will drag on the ground.
JEHANNE	Please, Sire.
CHARLES	It's an awesome responsibility. We quite like being the Dauphin. No one bothers us with stupid requests. But if we're King, well then, everything will be different. We'll have duties of state to contend with. Can't we just think about it for a while?
JEHANNE	The King of Heaven says you must be crowned this week.
CHARLES	The King of Heaven. Imagine George — an entire month without hearing of the King of Heaven and now he's back in full force.
GEORGE	The King of Heaven should take a vacation.
JEHANNE	*(starting to cry)* I do all this work and all you can do is sit back and make fun of me.
CHARLES	It wasn't our idea to raise the siege. None of this was our idea. Maybe, we don't like being dragged hither and yon.
JEHANNE	If you didn't have such fat friends, you'd be a lot more portable.
CHARLES	You shouldn't be rude to George. He makes a very dangerous enemy.

JEHANNE	I'd rather have him as an enemy than as a friend. He's an evil man.
GEORGE	I've had it up to the eyeballs with this little strumpet and her voices from Heaven. *(getting up)* Call me when she's gone. *(leaving)*
CHARLES	Jehanne, please stop crying. I hate to see women cry. I hate to see anyone cry, actually, but women seem to do it more than most.
JEHANNE	*(between sobs)* I don't think it's womanly to cry. I worked so hard and it's all to come to naught.
CHARLES	But it hasn't come to naught. You've revived our spirits. There's new blood in our veins. There's even colour in our cheeks. We must say, you don't look very well.
JEHANNE	I was wounded.
CHARLES	Lost a lot of blood on our behalf, did you?
JEHANNE	Some.
CHARLES	You must rest, then. Postpone the coronation till you feel better.
JEHANNE	No. You must be crowned as soon as possible.
CHARLES	And your Voices insist upon it?
JEHANNE	That's all they tell me. Over and over and over again. Crown the Dauphin. Crown the Dauphin.
CHARLES	Are you all right, Jehanne?
JEHANNE	I'm very tired, Sire. The voices won't leave me alone. You must be crowned this week.
CHARLES	Very well. We will miss you, Jehanne.
JEHANNE	But I'll be right beside you at the ceremony.

CHARLES So, you will. *(taking her hand)* It will be our consummation. Our little blood bond. *(sighing and getting up to leave)*

JEHANNE Something wrong, Sire?

CHARLES We didn't choose you, Jehanne. You chose yourself. *(leaving)*

> *MARGARET and CATHERINE leave with him. MICHAEL gives a little bow to JEHANNE before leaving. GILLES enters.*

GILLES Close your eyes.

> *JEHANNE closes her eyes. GILLES leaves, returns with cape.*

GILLES Open your eyes.

JEHANNE *(opening eyes)* Oh, it's beautiful!

GILLES You said you wanted a new costume. It's an exact replica of the cape Jehanne wore at the coronation. That was her zenith. Her time of glory. *(handing it to JEHANNE)* Put it on.

> *JEHANNE puts cape on.*

GILLES Yes, yes. *(going to stroke JEHANNE's head)*

JEHANNE *(pulling away)* You don't give a damn about me! You're just using me to pretend I'm her.

GILLES And what's wrong with that, François. We all have our illusions. I satisfy your illusion of being cherished and you satisfy mine.

JEHANNE But I want to be loved for myself.

GILLES Why should you be? What have you done to deserve it?

JEHANNE	Why do I have to do anything? Why can't I just be myself!
GILLES	The world doesn't work that way, François. You should know that. Next scene! *(turning around)* Who gave you that?
JEHANNE	You did. Just now.
GILLES	Next scene! Who gave you that?!
JEHANNE	Oh, sorry. The Duke of Alençon.
GILLES	Feeling. I want feeling. *(grabbing her)* You are Jehanne. Who gave you that!
JEHANNE	*(pulling away)* The Duke of Alençon. To thank me for raising the siege.
GILLES	You didn't raise the siege all by yourself, you know.
JEHANNE	Do you want a cape, too, Gilles? Isn't it beautiful! *(swirling around)*
GILLES	You spend a lot of time with him.
JEHANNE	I enjoy his company. He makes me laugh.
GILLES	I don't make you laugh.
JEHANNE	What do you have to do with it?
GILLES	You're wasting your time flirting with the Duke. He's married.
JEHANNE	That's never stopped any man I ever knew.
GILLES	What do you mean?
JEHANNE	I'm just making a joke.
GILLES	Don't. I hate it when you make those jokes.
JEHANNE	What jokes?

Act Two / 117

GILLES — Women's jokes. I've watched you with the other men. It's as though you're another person. Flirting. Smiling up at them. It's nauseating.

JEHANNE — Have you seen my scarf?

GILLES — You're not listening to me.

JEHANNE — Yes, I am. But I'm also trying to find my scarf. Have you seen it?

GILLES — I'm not your slave!

JEHANNE — I never asked you to be my slave. I'm asking you if you've seen my scarf.

GILLES — It's in your pocket.

JEHANNE — *(finding a red scarf)* Silly me. *(putting it on)*

GILLES — Who gave you that?

JEHANNE — La Hire.

GILLES — You're everybody's darling, aren't you.

JEHANNE — You sound like a jealous husband.

GILLES — Release me! I'm tired of being your dog's body. Release me from your spell.

JEHANNE — Most people never know what it's like to give their life to a higher cause. You should be honoured, Gilles. The voices have chosen you to serve me.

GILLES — I don't want to serve you.

JEHANNE — Someone has to look after the dark.

Lights come down slowly.

Scene Seven

> *Lights up. Gilles has gone. ISABELLE is standing off to one side. JEHANNE sees ISABELLE and gasps.*

ISABELLE Didn't expect to see me here, did you?

JEHANNE Maman? Is that you?

ISABELLE Of course it's me. Don't you even recognize your own mother?

JEHANNE You look different. Is Father with you?

ISABELLE No. I came alone.

JEHANNE It's a long way to travel by yourself.

ISABELLE You did it. Why shouldn't I? Your father and I were very worried about you. We didn't know what happened to you. Of course, your father had his ideas, which were less than comforting. Why didn't you send us a message from Chinon?

JEHANNE I had to prove myself worthy of you.

ISABELLE But why, Jeanette? I always knew you were a good girl.

Act Two / 119

JEHANNE — Please, Maman. Don't scold me. Be happy for me. *(showing off her cape)* Look! Isn't it beautiful! The Duke of Alençon gave it to me. I can't believe I actually did it. Charles is King!

ISABELLE — I am proud of you, Jeanette. It's a great honour that you were chosen. I wish you'd told me that the powers spoke to you. I would have been so happy.

JEHANNE — They told me not to tell anyone. Maybe they thought you would tell Father and he'd stop me from going. Keeping it to myself keeps the power stronger. I feel I lose some of it, each time I talk about it.

ISABELLE — There's no need to worry about your power. It will be time to come home soon.

JEHANNE — Why?

ISABELLE — You've done all you set out to do. It's time to go back to Domremy.

JEHANNE — What will I do there?

ISABELLE — You're going to have to resume a normal life, sometime.

JEHANNE — Why? This is my life. Here. I'm in charge of the army.

ISABELLE — They won't let you be in charge for long.

JEHANNE — Why not?

ISABELLE — You're a woman.

JEHANNE — It's a bit late to tell me that, Maman. I've done things no woman has ever done.

ISABELLE — You were a girl, then. You were neither male nor female.

JEHANNE   Doesn't anything I've done for the last year mean anything to you!

ISABELLE   All the things you've done! What about the powers!

JEHANNE   All right. They instruct me. But I do it. Maman, you always said women should be warriors. I'm a warrior.

ISABELLE   You're a vessel for the powers. You led the army because they inspired the men through you. But your time is almost over. You're turning into a woman. It's happening to you and you can't change it.

JEHANNE   Why should I lose my power just because I'm becoming a woman?

ISABELLE   You don't lose power. It changes. It needs to recover itself. It is in the nature of power to have cycles. You can't use power without replenishing yourself. Otherwise, it will turn against you. This particular cycle is ending.

JEHANNE   But I like it here. I don't want to go home.

ISABELLE   You like pretending you're a man.

JEHANNE   Why can't I be a man? I do everything they do.

ISABELLE   Jeanette, you have breasts.

JEHANNE   It's only my body. I should rise above my body. I'm trying not to need it, anymore. I don't need to eat the way I used to. I can hear my Voices better when I fast.

ISABELLE   If you deny your nature, you will destroy yourself. And Jeanette, you are denying that you are a woman.

JEHANNE I know why my Voices told me not to tell you about my mission. You're jealous. I'm doing everything you always wanted to do. I don't care what you say. I want to be a man and live as they do. I want the freedom to do as I please!

ISABELLE *(taking JEHANNE's hand)* Jeanette, you must return with me.

JEHANNE NO! I won't go back! I am not a woman! do you hear me! I am not a woman! *(running out)*

Scene Eight

JEHANNE and the two whores.
MICHAEL and CATHERINE.

WHORE 1 Oh, if it isn't the Blessed Virgin!

JEHANNE *(trying to push by them)* Get out of my way!

WHORE 2 Feeling crabby today, are we?

WHORE 1 Maybe we've got our curse . *(curtseying)*

WHORE 2 Oh no, the Maid of France doesn't get the curse. She's too pure for that. Haven't you heard?

WHORE 1 She doesn't get the curse? *(to WHORE 2)* Are you sure? *(to JEHANNE)* Is that true? How'd you manage that? Get in good with God.

JEHANNE I banned all of you from the camp.

WHORE 1 And the soldiers were kind enough to invite us back.

JEHANNE Leave this instant!

WHORE 2 Make us!

WHORE 1 Yeah, make us!

Act Two / 123

>*JEHANNE pulls out sword and brandishes it.*

WHORE 2 Oooooh. I'm really scared. Are you going to hit us with your sword?

JEHANNE YES! *(rushing at whores)*

>*WHORE 1 runs away. WHORE 2 turns to run. JEHANNE catches her. They fight. Jehanne cracks the sword across the whore's backside. The sword breaks.*

VOICE OF CATHERINE *(hissing)* You have struck one of our women with your sword.

WHORE 2 Aaaaw! You broke your sword. Aaw! Too bad. *(running off)*

JEHANNE *(in tears)* Catherine! Catherine!

>*The third VOICE appears. She is wrapped in a cloak. Her features are not visible.*

JEHANNE *(backing away)* NO!

MARGARET We are Margaret. We are the voice you could never see.

JEHANNE NO! Stay away from me!

MARGARET *(removing cloak from face)* We will help you bear children.

JEHANNE Catherine! I want Catherine!

MARGARET We will protect you from evil voices.

JEHANNE Michael, where are you! I want Catherine! I want Michael! I don't want you. Go away!! Oooooh! *(doubling over)*

MARGARET	Do not despair, Jehanne. We are weakened. You split the power, but perhaps, out of the severing, a new bond could be forged.
JEHANNE	Why do you look like my mother?
MARGARET	You're not seeing clearly, Jehanne.
JEHANNE	*(in tears)* You're not taking me back! Catherine! Where are you? Don't leave me! *(looking down, there is blood on her legs, and screaming)*

GILLES rushes over to JEHANNE.

GILLES	Jehanne! Jehanne! Are you all right?
JEHANNE	*(hysterical)* Get away from me!
GILLES	Jehanne!
JEHANNE	Stop calling me Jehanne. Jesus Christ! Why didn't anyone warn me about this!
GILLES	I wanted you to feel the way Jehanne felt.
JEHANNE	It was a mean trick.
GILLES	One of life's mysteries, François. Be thankful that it's just a trick and not for real.
JEHANNE	Sire?
GILLES	Yes.
JEHANNE	That last scene's wrong. Jehanne wanted to go back to Domremy.
GILLES	How would you know!
JEHANNE	I can feel her, sire.

GEORGE arrives, dressed as a bishop. He is carrying a stake.

Act Two / 125

GEORGE	Marshall. *(bowing)*
GILLES	Oh. I'd forgotten. We're going to rehearse the final scene. François, this is Bishop Cauchon, your prosecutor at the trial.
JEHANNE	The trial! You said we weren't going to—
GILLES	Don't worry, François. I'm not sure I even want to include this scene. It's just a rehearsal.
	CHARLES enters. He is wearing a half-mask. He is dressed in flowing white robes.
CHARLES	Gilles, darling!
GILLES	God, you look fabulous!
CHARLES	Oh, do you think so? I must say white becomes me.
JEHANNE	Why does he always get to play God?
CHARLES as GOD	Darling, when you're my age and you've been a faggot for as long as I have, you'll get to play God, too.
JEHANNE	Yeah, well, you don't do anything. You just sit on your ass all day.
GOD	Have to rest it, dearie. *(giggling)* Oh!
JEHANNE	Jesus, I hope I never become like that.
GOD	You won't live that long. *(to GILLES)* Did you tell him about the last scene? *(winking then singing)* Sing around the campfire. Be a campfire girl!
JEHANNE	OH NO! *(to GILLES)* You told me—
GILLES	He's just kidding, François.

GOD	What's black and comes on a stick?
GILLES	God, don't scare François. Now climb up to your cloud and behave yourself.
	GOD climbs up scaffold.
GOD	And I was having so much fun.
	The other actors enter. One of them is carrying a torch. He stands beside GEORGE/CAUCHON.
GILLES	Good. We have the townspeople. Now, we can begin.
	The actors move toward JEHANNE/FRANÇOIS and try to take him to the stake. He struggles.
JEHANNE	No, please.
GILLES	*(clapping hands)* BEGIN!
CAUCHON	*(to JEHANNE)* Do you dare to change your confession! You say here that you have lied about your Voices. It is written:
JEHANNE	*(whining to GILLES)* Sire, please—
CAUCHON	"I, Jehanne, abjure, detest, deny and entirely renounce and separate myself from my crimes and my errors. I have blasphemed God and his saints."
JEHANNE	No! It's not true. I take it all back. All that I said, I did only because of fear of the fire.
	GILLES and other actors look slightly puzzled. JEHANNE / FRANÇOIS is not saying what he's supposed to say.
JEHANNE	You are a false preacher. My Voices are from Heaven!

Act Two / 127

CAUCHON	How dare you put yourself between man and God. You shall burn for this! *(grabbing torch and thrusts it at JEHANNE)*
	JEHANNE screams and faints.
GOD	Is he going to do that every time we do the scene?
	JEHANNE comes to and looks around.
JEHANNE	Where am I? *(staring at GILLES)* You!
CAUCHON	Deny your voices or you will burn! *(pushing torch at JEHANNE)*
JEHANNE	*(pushing it back)* I am not afraid of your fire, anymore. I have been through your fires. I brought you the finest help that was ever brought to knight or to city. And it was the help of the King of Heaven! *(raising eyes, seeing GOD)* And the King of Heaven does not look like that!
	GOD looks bewildered.
JEHANNE	He's not a wise old man, sitting on a cloud. My voices — Saint Catherine, Saint Margaret — women's voices. Even the Archangel Michael was a woman. That's why I could never describe my voices. No one would follow me if I told them they were women. You've made your own world here, Gilles. It's of, for and about men. Even I am a man in your creation.
GILLES	You wanted it that way. You never wanted to be a woman.
JEHANNE	Women have only one use in your world. Kindling for your fires. You betrayed me, Gilles. You betrayed me to your male God.
GILLES	Your saints betrayed you. Where were they when you needed them? They led you into the fire. You and I both knew that was your destiny.

JEHANNE You and Charles decided that was my destiny. You deserted me, Gilles. I was not prepared to die. The burning. The flames tearing into my flesh. I did not die for a very long time, Gilles. I wanted to die, but I couldn't. My heart, the centre of it all, would not burn. Even now, I still feel the pain because my heart contains it. Your lust for power has caused this.

GILLES Don't talk to me about power. You thrived on your power. You made me your slave. Your life was sacrificed for a mighty cause.

JEHANNE As yours will be, too. But for my cause. Not yours.

GILLES You don't understand. New power has been forged from the merging of the two religions. My Christian mystery play is also an ancient invocation. And it worked. I knew it would. You came just as I'd hoped.

JEHANNE You didn't invoke me, Gilles. I came because I felt like it. And don't think you can do it again. Maybe, it's your imagination playing tricks on you. Maybe, you're going mad. Maybe, all this power you're hoarding and collecting is finally going to turn against you.

GILLES Stay with me, please Jehanne. I'm part of you and I want you near me.

JEHANNE *(laughing)* You want me, do you? Then, share my pain, Gilles. Share my pain. *(touching him)*

GILLES Aaaagh! I'm burning.

JEHANNE The wind will change! *(collapsing)*

> *Wind blows harder and harder. GOD is blown off the scaffold.*

GOD OW! JESUS CHRIST!

Act Two / 129

GILLES I'm burning! The fire! No! Don't touch me! Don't touch me! *(rolling around the ground, trying to beat off the flames)*

The other actors watch him.

GEORGE Marshall?

GILLES *(dazed)* What am I doing here? *(seeing torch)* Aaah! Put that torch out!

ACTOR *(with torch)* Sorry. *(exiting)*

GEORGE Are you all right? François has fainted and God fell out of Heaven.

GOD My bum's killing me. I've had enough for one day. *(leaving)*

GEORGE Should we continue?

GILLES No. No, please go. We'll be all right.

The actors leave.

GILLES *(bending down, patting JEHANNE on the cheek)* Jehanne?

JEHANNE opens her eyes, sits up groggily.

GILLES You see me now in my shame, Jehanne.

JEHANNE Sire?

GILLES You should have come when I first did my play for you. *(stroking JEHANNE's head)* My Mystery of the Siege of Orleans. Five hundred and sixty three actors. All new costumes. The finest silk and velvet. Virgin cloth. I was certain I could summon you. A six month spectacle for the town of Orleans. But you never came.

JEHANNE   Sire, please. She's dead. I'm François. *(getting up, starting to walk away)*

GILLES   *(catching JEHANNE's arm)* You want to know why you'll never be a martyr, don't you, François?

JEHANNE   Sire, I don't even know what a martyr is. *(pulling away from GILLES)*

GILLES   *(maintaining his grip on JEHANNE)* You want to know why I never ransomed you, don't you? *(laughing and pulling out a gold coin then dangles it in front of JEHANNE)* Do you see this gold coin? *(standing behind JEHANNE)*

JEHANNE   I don't want to do this, sire.

GILLES   You've done it, before. *(fondling JEHANNE)* Admit it. You enjoy this. I wouldn't do this to you if you didn't enjoy it.

JEHANNE takes the coin.

GILLES   Why didn't you come, before? Are you angry with me? It had to be done. There was no other way. *(continuing to fondle JEHANNE)* The secret of power is in the blood, François. *(pulling out a red handkerchief and tying JEHANNE's hands behind her back)* Blood was needed for the sacrifice. We argued about this many times. Jehanne and I. *(pulling out another handkerchief and gagging JEHANNE)*

JEHANNE looks startled.

GILLES   The Old Ways forbade the shedding of blood. *(pulling out a knife and plays with it in front of JEHANNE's face)* Why are the Christians now in power? You don't have to answer that. It's the blood sacrament. Christ and his disciples. We have to move with the times. We can't deny that the Christian Church is in control. And they got their power from the sacrament. Jehanne said that

GILLES	*(continued)* I was perverting the Old Religion. That I was turning it into sorcery. But even with the power of her voices, she couldn't deny that she was the Divine Sacrifice. *(pulling knife against JEHANNE's throat)* Blood was needed and it had to be innocent blood. Her blood. *(taking knife away)* Your blood isn't innocent, François. And that's why you'll never be a martyr.
	JEHANNE falls forward in relief.
GILLES	Only a victim. *(pulling JEHANNE's head up and raising the knife)*
	Blackout. Lights up. GILLES DE RAIS is alone on stage.
GILLES	I got it all wrong. I worshipped the woman and fucked the man. That is not the way it is done. That is not the way it is done at all!
	The PRIEST, GEORGE, CHARLES, MICHAEL and CATHERINE enter.
PRIEST	*(to GILLES)* Have you seen François?
GILLES	No.
GEORGE	He's been gone for days.
GILLES	Boys. They're restless and they run off.
CATHERINE	I think we should try and find him. *(leaving, calling for FRANÇOIS)*
MICHAEL	I'll help you. *(leaving)* François!
	GEORGE, CHARLES and the PRIEST leave, calling for FRANÇOIS.

GILLES Is the present always so bleak that people are willing to sacrifice what they have for the promise of a better future? The Christian Church was my promise. I believed in it. It constituted order — a well-ordered hierarchy with man at the top. You're probably thinking — Christianity is over and done with. Why flog a dead horse? Well, in my time, it was just entering into its prime. So, I presume, if Christianity is on the wane, then another system is on the ascendant. Making lots of promises. My advice to you is — Don't believe it. Even when you see it, don't believe it. There's a rug being pulled out from under every man every minute.

Scene Nine

ISABELLE enters with JEHANNE. She is wearing a dress. She looks very mature and sophisticated.

GILLES turns and sees them and gasps.

ISABELLE See, Jeanette. He's overjoyed to see you.

JEHANNE Gilles!

GILLES *(pulling out a cross and holding it up to JEHANNE)* Get away from me!

ISABELLE What's the matter, Marshall de Rais? You are a Marshall, now. They promoted you well. Isn't that exciting, Jeanette? Your friend, Gilles, is now a Field Marshall.

JEHANNE That's wonderful news, Gilles.

GILLES stares at her.

ISABELLE Marshall? Are you all right?

GILLES Please. *(pause)* Send her away.

ISABELLE   But why, Marshall? Isn't your little presentation here designed to invoke my daughter's spirit. Et puis voila! Here she is. But flesh and blood, Marshall. Nothing ethereal about Jeanette. Touch her if you don't believe me. Come Jeanette, put out your arm.

JEHANNE holds out her arm to Gilles.

GILLES   *(backing away)* That woman is not Jehanne.

JEHANNE   Oh Gilles, how can you say such cruel things. I thought you of all people would acknowledge me. I suppose I have to prove myself. I know your secret name.

GILLES looks puzzled.

JEHANNE   Bluebeard.

GILLES   Oh. *(pause)* Yes, I was once called Bluebeard.

ISABELLE   And so you shall again.

GILLES   I'd rather not. I never liked the name. Madame, take your impostor away. She wearies me.

ISABELLE   You turn your back on Jeanette.

GILLES   Jehanne was burned at the stake. You know that. I know that. Everyone in France knows that. *(gesturing to JEHANNE)* Except for her, of course. I think you'd better enlighten her. *(to JEHANNE)* Your breasts are too large. That's what gives you away.

ISABELLE   Jeanette didn't die. Her breasts are large because she's now a woman. She's not your boy, anymore.

GILLES   I beg you. Please leave me. Your daughter is dead.

ISABELLE	You weren't there. How do you know! Did you see her burn?
GILLES	No.
ISABELLE	You did nothing to save her. You, with all your wealth—
GILLES	Please!
ISABELLE	Someone did save her. Her noble and true friend, the Duke of Alencon. He arranged it so they burned another girl in her place.
GILLES	A life was taken, just the same. Some poor girl suffered the torments of the damned and worse yet, for something she hadn't done.
ISABELLE	What had Jeanette done to deserve such a fate?
GILLES	I don't know, Madame, but it was her fate. The Jehanne I knew would have had the courage to meet it. What do you want from me? Why are you here?
ISABELLE	I want you to give back what you have stolen from my daughter.
GILLES	And what is that, pray?
ISABELLE	Her womanhood. You stole it from her and you shall pay it back tenfold.
GILLES	I can't do anything about your daughter now. And she! *(pointing to JEHANNE)* She is a travesty.
ISABELLE	I want justice.
GILLES	You can't have justice but I imagine you will settle for money. *(fumbling in pockets, pulling rings off fingers)* I don't have much but I'll give you what I have. Anything. Please. Just get out of my sight.

ISABELLE We'll take your money, Marshall and we'll have justice, too.

> *ISABELLE and JEHANNE curtsey and leave. The actor playing GEORGE enters. He is dressed as a bishop. He could also make his announcements from the back of the theatre, thus not being entirely visible to the audience.*

GEORGE MARSHALL GILLES DE RAIS. YOU ARE UNDER ARREST.

GILLES What for?

GEORGE Charges of assaulting an officer of the Church, charges of heresy. Do you put yourself under the jurisdiction of the Church.

PRIEST *(entering)* It's a trap, Gilles. Don't do it.

GILLES I'm no heretic. I'm as good a Catholic as these bishops. I will face these charges.

> *CHARLES can also be at the back of the theatre. He is dressed as a bishop.*

CHARLES Marshall Gilles de Rais, you are charged as follows:

GEORGE ITEM. That Gilles de Rais, the accused, entered into a pact with evil spirits by which he agreed to their will — in this pact, the accused entreated the evil spirits to furnish him with knowledge, wealth and power and this has been, and is, true.

GILLES I don't have much money or power, now.

CHARLES That is irrelevant.

GILLES So, I practiced the art of alchemy. Is the pursuit of knowledge an evil occupation?

GEORGE Did you or did you not conjure spirits?

Act Two / 137

GILLES I tried but they wouldn't come to me. No. I didn't promise my soul or my life. I simply wanted the knowledge and the power to control the mysteries.

CHARLES Heretic! Only God controls the mysteries.

GEORGE ITEM. That during the past 14 years, the accused has murdered one hundred and forty or more innocent boys and girls in the castles of Chamtoc, Tiffauges and Machecoul.

GILLES WHAT! MURDERED?!

CHARLES ITEM. That the accused, with various of his accomplices has cut the throats of, killed, massacred in odious fashion various innocent boys.

GILLES I DENY THESE MURDERS! WHY ARE YOU ACCUSING ME OF SUCH THINGS?!

CHARLES That he has practiced with these children the lewdness that is against nature — the vice of sodomy.

GILLES Ah! That's the crux of it. Where would we be without our scapegoats. Worship the man and fuck the woman. One simple law and I failed to grasp it.

GEORGE ITEM.

CHARLES ITEM.

GILLES *(to GEORGE and CHARLES)* Hypocrites! You raging towering hypocrites! You — my judges?! I'd rather be hung by a lynch mob than judged by the likes of you! *(to PRIEST)* And you, Father! How could you allow them to accuse me of such things.

CATHERINE and MICHAEL enter as two mothers.

CATHERINE My boy. He wasn't very bright, but he was dear to me. I wanted to see him get ahead. So, when one of the Marshall's men asked to buy my child, I saw there was no other way for us to survive. So, I sold him to the Marshall.

GILLES You sold your child! What sort of mother are you!

CATHERINE A poor one.

MICHAEL We were very poor. My boy was very beautiful. He was the only chance we had. The Marshall's servant said he would give me the 100 sous I badly needed for a new dress if I would give him my boy. He came back with the money but there were 20 sous missing. He promised me 100 and he only gave me 80. I knew he wouldn't keep his other promises. The Marshall is an evil man.

CATHERINE I only got 60 sous for my Colin.

MICHAEL Your Colin wasn't as pretty as my Pierre.

MARGARET *(entering)* I didn't sell my son. He went to beg at the castle and was never seen again. I told him not to go there. I told him it was the Castle of Death.

GILLES These women are lying. They've been paid to testify against me.

WOMEN Where do all our children go, then? They run away and they never come home.

GILLES They grow up. You're looking for children who don't exist anymore.

WOMEN You killed them!

GILLES I deny it. I deny all these charges.

Act Two / 139

GEORGE CONFESS!

JEHANNE enters, or it can simply be JEHANNE's voice which is heard.

JEHANNE Confess, Gilles!

GILLES *(turning to JEHANNE)* No! These are false charges! They can burn me for being what I am. I will be proud to die as their scapegoat. Let the world know why they killed me!

JEHANNE You must pay back what you have taken. I went to the stake for telling the truth. You must go for telling a lie.

GEORGE & CHARLES Will you confess!

GILLES NO!

JEHANNE Make it a big lie, Gilles. It is your mission. *(exiting)*

GILLES I wanted what you had and now I've got it. All of it. *(laughing then announcing)* MY CONFESSION.

NOTE: GILLES' confession must be delivered in such a way that one is absolutely convinced that he did, in fact, murder the children.

Yes. I killed your children. I sodomized them and then I killed them. I cut their little heads off and I put them up on pikes. I chopped their arms and legs off and I and my servants judged which limbs were the prettiest. There was nothing I liked better than to seduce the child who came to my castle. I dressed him in beautiful clothes. I gave him figs and pomegranates. I watched his eyes fill with desire. I whispered sweet and sensual flatteries in his ear. And in the moment of his greatest happiness, I slit his throat.

GILLES *(continued)* The greedy ones, I confess, I tormented. I don't like avaricious children, so I would tease them a little before killing them. And if an ugly child accompanied the one I fancied — well, I would have my pleasure with the pretty one. But I felt it my moral responsibility to kill the ugly one as well, so he would not pine for his friend. Loneliness is a terrible thing. *(pause)* I confess I am an evil man and I have done diabolical things for no motive, other than my own pleasure. I am your monster.

PRIEST I must protest. I can't believe you did these things.

GILLES Alas, Father, you torment yourself and me as well.

PRIEST I do not torment myself. I am quite simply astonished. Please. I want to know the pure truth.

GILLES There was no other reason. I have told you worse things than the truth itself. Enough to send ten thousand men to their death.

CHARLES and GEORGE take GILLES to the stake. They tie him there. The women fetch kindling.

GILLES I implore the mercy and pardon of my creator as well as the mercy and pardon of the relatives and friends of the children I have so cruelly massacred. You, whoever you are, whom I have sinned-against and injured, I beg the succour of your Christian prayers. I beg your forgiveness.

CATHERINE carries a lighted torch.
CATHERINE We forgive you, Gilles.

MICHAEL *(carrying a torch)* Yes. We forgive you.

GILLES Saint Michael, will you talk to me, now? I pray you. Receive and commend my soul to God.

Act Two / 141

They light the stake. Flames, then blackout.

Lights up on the actress playing JEHANNE. She should be wearing a mourning veil — something to disguise her appearance.

MARIE My name is Marie de Rais. Gilles de Rais was my father. I never knew him. I don't know whether he killed all those children. Nobody has since mentioned his crimes. It's as though they never happened. King Charles annulled his debts and restored his lands. My suitors are unconcerned. They seem more than willing to court the daughter of a murderer. My fortune makes them turn a blind eye. I have not had a happy life. I've had one moment of peace — one glimpse of the way things might be. One night, I was asleep and this Voice woke me up. It said, "Marie, you are the Goddess of Creation. Go! Go to the pyre where your father was burned. Go and erect a fountain to Saint Marie — the Milk Goddess." The Voice woke me up every night with the same command till I finally did what it said. I dedicated the fountain to Saint Marie but everyone prays to my father. All the barren women in the village pray to Saint Gilles to be made fertile. Pregnant women ask Saint Gilles for plentiful milk for their babies. They say my father is returning the lives he took. The people of Nantes love my father. Every year, in honour of his death, they come to his shrine and they beat their children. I stopped hearing the Voice shortly after I built the fountain. It makes me very sad. I miss my Voice. I realize my talking of milk and child — birth is a bit of a letdown from what you're used to. No battles. No blood. Just the simple continuance of the human race.

The End.

A Woman's Comedy

by Beth Herst

Beth Herst was born in Toronto and educated in Toronto and London, England. She holds a Ph.D. in English Literature from the University of London. In addition to several plays, she is author of *The Dickens Hero*, a study of the novels of Charles Dickens. Beth Herst lives in Toronto where she is currently a Writer-in-Residence at the Tarragon Theatre.

Introduction by Ann Wilson

Angeline Goreau's 1980 book called *Reconstructing Aphra* begins: "Aphra Behn existed. If she had not, we would have had to invent her." The hyperbolic claim attests to the attraction which feminists feel to the Restoration playwright whose life, by any standard, is remarkable. Born in 1640, Behn and her family visited the British colony of Surinam in 1663. Her experiences during her year-long stay there became the basis for one of her best-known works, the novel *Oroonoko*. When she returned to London, she married a merchant who died during the plague. It would seem the terms of his will had not been established, and that Behn was left without an income — an all too familiar story even now — and was forced to support herself. Eschewing what for women of her generation would have been the more conventional route of remarriage, Behn became a spy for the British government which sent her to Antwerp to monitor troop movements during the Dutch wars. Once there, the government did not pay her and so she had to borrow money for her return passage. On her return to London in 1667, she found a city which had been virtually destroyed by the Great Fire and, as a consequence of the tremendous costs of rebuilding, was financially unstable. Money lenders were unwilling to extend credit and so Behn, unable to repay her debts, was sent to prison. Soon after her release, she began her career as a playwright, writing a range of successful plays including *The Forced Marriage, The Rover, The City Heiress,* and *The Lucky Chance.*

Unlike many of her generation who wrote for the stage in their leisure, Behn wrote for money, describing herself as "'an author who is forced to write for bread and is not ashamed to own it'" (quoted in Case

36). Her plays were successful, causing some of her contemporaries to sneer that she was less interested in artistic achievement than in financial success. What is remarkable about Behn is that through her writing, she was able to maintain her independence. Virginia Woolf celebrated her in *A Room of One's Own*, writing that Aphra Behn had to make her own way by living by her wits. She had to work on equal terms with men. She made, by working very hard, enough to live on. The importance of that fact outweighs anything that she actually wrote. For now that Aphra Behn had done it, girls could go to their parents and say, "You need not give me an allowance; I can make money by my pen." (95-96)

Aphra Behn's struggle to maintain her independence in an age in which women were expected to marry, and so to be financially dependent on a man, has strong and immediate correspondences with the lives of women today. While it is easy to understand why feminists often represent her as a precursor to the women's movement in the twentieth century, we should be careful that the luxury of hindsight does not blind us to what must have been a life of enormous struggle and pain. Beth Herst's *A Woman's Comedy* poignantly charts the contradictions in Behn's life.

In *A Woman's Comedy*, while Aphra Behn secures an income as a playwright, the demands of writing for the stage force her to compromise her vision. When she gives her new manuscript to Harcourt, a theatre manager, he refuses it, complaining that:

"Your heroine misused, betrayed, attacked on every side. Left alone at the last, neither widow, maid nor wife. And yet she lives on, past the final act. The Town will not countenance such a moral. It violates all rules of form." Behn replies, "Life again, sir, brings the same complaint. It rarely observes the decorums of art."

The failure of life to conform to the rules is one with which Behn is familiar: in her own life, she rarely observed the rules of social decorum. Nowhere is this refusal more pronounced than in her relationship with Jack Hoyle.

When Behn first meets Hoyle she is walking through the park, her face masked, apparently one of her few concessions to the social conventions of her day. Hoyle and Behn initiate their affair through what is ostensibly a discussion of her writing. He offers to play whatever role she writes for him, but is reluctant to play either comedy or tragedy because "one must always finish in marriage, the other in death." Behn offers to revise dramatic form, prompting Hoyle to comment, "You break forms at your peril, and run the risk of being damned for the attempt." When Hoyle claims to "scorn disguise" preferring the bare face which it hides, Behn lowers her mask and comments, "Then, sir, you deceive yourself more than disguise could do. This is the veriest mask of all."

This moment raises one of the questions in *A Woman's Comedy:* can an individual be truly free from the determination of social forces, able to reveal her true face? Initially, Behn seems to have found in Hoyle a man who is sympathetic to her desire to remain independent and who wants to enjoy a relationship with her as an equal. Hoyle, the son of a man who was implicated in the killing of Charles I and who then committed suicide, is himself an outsider. As Sir William Archer comments, "They're well-matched...He has no honour and she no shame." Although Hoyle and Behn initially appear to be well-suited, Herst does not depict their relationship sentimentally as the meeting of a man and a woman each of whom finds in the other a kindred spirit. There are clear parallels between the two inasmuch as each flouts social codes: Behn insists that she not be indebted to a man with whom she is involved sexually, while Hoyle is bisexual in a society in which homosexual acts are criminal. But despite sharing a certain rebelliousness, the two lovers are propelled by fundamentally different erotic investments. Although Behn accepts Hoyle's homosexual impulses, even offering to be sodomized by him so that she can better understand him, what she fails to understand is the degree to which Hoyle eroticizes the illegality of his desire for sex with boys. As if he yearns to be punished, his homosexual encounters are in public places — in the theatre, on the street — where he risks being found. And, to further complicate matters, these public spaces are contaminated by the plague so that he not only risks arrest, but also death. It would be difficult to argue that Hoyle's sexuality, expressed in ways which invite criminal prosecution and perhaps death, is free from an internalized social censure.

In the course of the play, it is similarly unclear that Behn ever fully understands Hoyle despite her love for him. What is sadly ironic is that they may have more in common than either ever understands, for she also lives under the spectre of death. When she explains to Hoyle that she writes because her husband's death left her penniless, she adds that her writing is an investment that she will "never be erased. Not entirely. Some faint mark will always remain behind and that will be my sign. My story." And like Hoyle, whose sexuality expresses a complex negotiation of innate sexual desire which is shaped by the forces of the society in which he lives, Aphra Behn herself is never entirely free of these forces. While she resists the urge to enjoy greater financial success by masking her identity through the signature of a masculine pseudonym and insists on her independence by refusing to be a nobleman's mistress, she nevertheless is willing to ask Hoyle to return the love letters which she has written to him so that she can publish them. Behn has earlier told Hoyle she writes "whatever I can sell"; in selling her letters to him, she seems to come perilously close to selling herself in order to survive.

A Woman's Comedy is a remarkable exploration of the complex intersections of social, sexual and financial economies in which all of us, like Aphra Behn, live. While the play is not, strictly speaking, a history — it expands upon and revises the facts of Aphra Behn's life — the impulses behind *A Woman's Comedy* are not so far removed from those of more conventional modes of historical writing. The attraction of history is always the relation between the past and the present: the need to know the past arises from the desire to understand the present. Aphra Behn's story is one which resonates with the concerns of our day, providing a moving, troubling and triumphant tale of a woman's struggle.

Works Cited:Case, Sue Ellen. *Feminism and Theatre*. London: Macmillan, 1988.
Goreau, Angeline. *Reconstructing Aphra: A Social Biography*. New York: Dial P., 1980.
Woolf, Virginia. *A Room of One's Own*. London: Hogarth Press, 1929.

Ann Wilson
November, 1993, University of Guelph

Production History

A Woman's Comedy was first performed April 1, 1992 at the Tarragon Theatre, Toronto, with the following cast:

APHRA BEHN	*Susan Coyne*
JACK HOYLE	*Randy Hughson*
BETTY LACY	*Donna Goodhand*
LORD GREVILLE	*Michael Hanrahan*
MR. HARCOURT	*John Gilbert*
SIR WILLIAM ARCHER	*Hume Baugh*

Directed by Urjo Kareda and Andy McKim.
Set and costume design by Sue LePage and Glenn Davidson.
Lighting by Glenn Davidson.

The Setting and Time

The backdrop to *A Woman's Comedy* is London in the 1670s and 1680s, that is, during the last two decades of the life of the historical Aphra Behn. No attempt has been made, however, to follow the strict chronology of her life, where it is known, or to establish a "real" timeframe for the events the play imagines. The world of the play is a self-consciously theatrical one. Characters walk out of one time and place and into another, as they walk out of one scene and into another. Though breaks between scenes have been indicated for convenience, the action is designed to be continuous.

A Woman's Comedy is neither a history nor a biography. It is a speculation, inspired by the life of the playwright Aphra Behn.

The Characters

APHRA BEHN
JACK HOYLE
BETTY LACY
LORD GREVILLE
MR. HARCOURT
SIR WILLIAM ARCHER

Prologue

N.B. All scenes flow from one to the next without a break in the action. Music. APHRA stands, masked.

APHRA "The late ingenious Mrs. Behn. Author of diverse plays, poems and other works. Died the sixteenth day of April in the year sixteen hundred and eighty-nine.

Here lies a proof that wit can never be
Defence enough against mortality."

(lowering her mask) I could have written better verses myself. I did write better verses myself. It is Westminster Abbey, if you wondered. But not Poets' Corner. A plain black slab in the eastern cloister. Outside. Easy to overlook, perhaps, but not entirely removed. A sort of waiting-room for Parnassus, where the underrated and the ignored dwell in the hope of a very uncertain resurrection.

HOYLE and GREVILLE enter.

APHRA I never thought they'd let me get this close. Critics are so much less forgiving than God.

APHRA raises her mask, exits. HOYLE and GREVILLE lift glasses in a toast. They are in a tavern.

Act One, Scene One

HOYLE   To your lordship's welcome return to Town.

GREVILLE   Welcome, indeed. I am almost dead for a sight of St. James's.

HOYLE   You do not love rustic retirement, my lord? No taste for pastoral pleasures or sylvan shades?

GREVILLE   There's something to be said for country cunt, I concede. For the rest, I'd sooner be buried alive. But business, Jack. Business.

HOYLE   And what say the lady's friends? Am I to wish you joy? Will it be a match?

GREVILLE   Damn 'em, they haggle still for settlement and jointure, and barter as shrewdly as any merchants on the 'Change. Still, I think 'twill come to terms soon enough.

HOYLE   But the lady herself?

GREVILLE   Aye? What of her?

HOYLE   Has she qualities? Beauty? Grace? Wit?

GREVILLE   She has a swingeing fortune, sir. That's more to the purpose. The rest I may lay in elsewhere.

HOYLE	A most convenient arrangement. I drink, my lord, to holy matrimony.
GREVILLE	You spoil good wine with such a theme. Pray, change the subject. What news of the Town this great age?
HOYLE	Why, sir, we wear on as ever. Hypocrisy is yet in fashion and truth-telling still a crime.
GREVILLE	Well, this is no news at all.

ARCHER enters.

GREVILLE	Here comes one will give me fresher intelligence. He is a walking gazette. D'you know him, Jack?
HOYLE	Not I, my lord.
GREVILLE	A most industrious collector of scandal. Sir William, I am glad to see you, sir.
ARCHER	My lord, you are most welcome back. *(addressing HOYLE)* Sir.
GREVILLE	Gentlemen, I must make you acquainted.
ARCHER	Servant to command.
HOYLE	Sir, yours.
GREVILLE	Mr. Hoyle, you must know, is a great railer against the age, and so I warn you. A misanthrope and confirmed hater of our poor wicked world.
ARCHER	A man just after my heart, my lord. It is a wicked world, sir. Gad, so 'tis. Full of nothing but fops and coxcombs. I can scarce bear it two days together. A silly, vain, idle world. Damn me if it isn't.
GREVILLE	You say nothing, Jack. And here a man of your very own humour too.

HOYLE	When fools are ever talking, a wise man holds his tongue.
ARCHER	Now that's well said, sir. "When fools are ever talking."
GREVILLE	Well said, indeed. But come, Sir William, what news of the Town? You are always the first in intelligence.
ARCHER	Sir, your most obedient. There's nothing spoken of now but this she-author, whose plays come on at the Duke's theatre.
GREVILLE	*She-author?* That's false grammar. What new monster's this?
ARCHER	Damn me, I have forgot the name. They sometimes call her *Astraea*, I know.
GREVILLE	*Astraea?*
HOYLE	Or Mrs. Behn, perhaps, sir?
ARCHER	The very name. I would have come to it myself directly.
GREVILLE	You know of her too, Jack?
HOYLE	Only as much as the rest of the Town. And that's little enough, if the truth were told. She writes plays, and publishes 'em too, and so keeps herself.
GREVILLE	An author in petticoats who writes for her keep? This is some strange hermaphrodite.
ARCHER	True. Your lordship says true. A monster, indeed. Gad, women write plays? They deserve to be burnt.
GREVILLE	The women or the plays?
ARCHER	Both, sure.

Act One / 155

HOYLE   I have seen this piece they talk of.

ARCHER   And so have I too. For novelty's sake.

HOYLE   The lady has a pretty wit.

GREVILLE   If the lady has a pretty face, she may make the better bargain for it.

ARCHER   No lady at all, sirs. That's certain. A country barber's spawn, who learnt her trick of scribbling in a debtors' jail, and sold much else before she came to selling plays. Or so they say.

HOYLE   A gentleman's daughter, sir, I heard.

ARCHER   Well. Married a Dutch merchant, buried him, then went a spy to Holland in the late war. That I know is true. The story's told on every side.

GREVILLE   A widow too? And an author? And a spy? This is an apparition to wonder at. I must positively view this comet.

HARCOURT enters.

GREVILLE   And there, gentlemen, stand our means. Mr. Harcourt, you come pat upon your cue. There's actor in your very bones, I think.

HARCOURT   My lord. I had not heard you were returned to Town.

GREVILLE   But newly arrived, and just now meaning to send to you to the playhouse.

HARCOURT   If I can be of service...

GREVILLE   Why, so you shall. But you must take some wine first.

HARCOURT   Thank you, my lord. Sirs.

A Woman's Comedy / 156

HARCOURT pours himself wine, drinks.

GREVILLE Mr. Manager, your playhouse has been making some stir, I find. I have been hearing strange tales since my return.

ARCHER Aye, aye, the woman's comedy, Mr. Harcourt. I have informed his lordship of all particulars.

HARCOURT Sir.

GREVILLE You must know, I am resolved to see this phenomenon.

ARCHER And so am I too. I have long meant to do so, I assure you.

GREVILLE Now, where shall I find her, sir? And when?

ARCHER That's the question, you see, sir.

HARCOURT I could not undertake to say for certain.

GREVILLE No, Mr. Harcourt?

HARCOURT She does not...You might perhaps find her at the playhouse. If your lordship cares to look so far.

GREVILLE So I will, and think to do some business there, while I'm about it. I am in the market for some fresh diversion. Your house has always a fair stock in hand. But something sound, and easily secured. I have had my fill of wooing. You understand me, sir?

HARCOURT Perfectly, my lord.

GREVILLE Then we must detain you here no longer. Pray, keep places for us in the pit this afternoon.

HARCOURT My lord. Sirs.

HARCOURT exits.

ARCHER That's a wondrous civil gentleman, sir. For a player.

HOYLE Most obliging, truly, sir.

ARCHER He plays the wild gallants and tragic lovers, you know, and does 'em the best I ever saw.

HOYLE Those are not his only parts, I think.

ARCHER Sir?

GREVILLE Will you quarrel with the poor players now? Faith, Jack, you are too severe. They at least make no secret of their pretence.

HOYLE Nor of their pimping neither.

GREVILLE They are paid to please.

HOYLE And 'twould be simple in them indeed to offend their best patrons in the pit. Would it not, sir?

ARCHER Truly, we may send a play to the devil any time we choose. If we Wits condemn it, you know, there is no appeal.

GREVILLE Well, Sir William, today we must temper judgment with mercy. In kindness to her sex, we'll spare the lady author the rigour of our wit.

ARCHER And so we will.

GREVILLE Now, sirs, I think 'tis high time to dine.

ARCHER At my charge, my lord. If you will do me the honour. The French house, perhaps?

GREVILLE Sir, your servant. Jack, d'you go?

HOYLE I'll follow you presently, my lord. Sir.

Music. GREVILLE and ARCHER exit. HOYLE lingers to finish his wine before following. Time shift. HARCOURT enters the theatre. He sits, begins to count the day's receipts. BETTY sweeps in, still "high" from the afternoon's triumph. She mimes an elaborate curtain call to imagined uproarious applause. APHRA enters carrying some manuscript, sees BETTY, laughs.

Two

BETTY What, my dear author, are you so impatient?

HARCOURT And the takings from your benefit still to be counted?

APHRA I could scarcely wait so long. Another hour would have killed me quite. Now quickly, pray, what sort of house?

HARCOURT I cannot remember a third day so full.

BETTY Boxes, pit and gallery. You are simply a greater novelty —

APHRA — than a two-headed cow, or any other such prodigy of nature. 'Tis good news, then?

HARCOURT One hundred pounds of good news, and house charges paid. For an author's day you could scarce do better.

APHRA That's more than I hoped.

HARCOURT But not more than you deserve.

BETTY It was a triumph.

APHRA I must thank you and your playing for it.

BETTY · Nay, if one cow cannot help her fellow. You must write me another part, just the same.

APHRA · Must I so? Well, I am about it now.

BETTY · *(taking manuscript from her)* Is this it?

APHRA · No.

BETTY · No, I see it is not.

APHRA · The other is almost ready. Only I fear you will think it too much like the last.

HARCOURT · Impossible, I can assure you.

APHRA · Sir?

HARCOURT · Having found the trick, keep to it, by all means. There's no more certain way of pleasing.

APHRA · Not even fresh fancies? Or new designs?

HARCOURT · 'Tis much more difficult. And less sure.

BETTY · For you see, that would force your audience to think, and there's nothing they come to a play less willing to do.

APHRA · Well, I may vary the form at least. May I not?

BETTY · A little way perhaps may pass. Mr. Harcourt, what say you?

HARCOURT · But never so far as confounds expectation.

BETTY · Very true. You must make your heroine young, witty, and handsome.

HARCOURT · And your hero a wild, rakish cavalier.

APHRA · A captain, for choice. Or a penniless younger son?

BETTY	You know the Town will not let us play anything else.
HARCOURT	'Tis set down. I must be sparkish and free, keep a company of mistresses, and take as many more before the plot is done.
BETTY	While I, some...
APHRA	Country heiress, run away from her friends —
HARCOURT	— who would match her with a fool —
APHRA	— she cannot love.
BETTY	Just. Now, I keep my virtue unquestioned till the final act. Then he declares his love. I confess mine.
APHRA	And finish all with a wedding.
HARCOURT	And a dance.
APHRA	But Mrs. Betty must be got into breeches too?
HARCOURT	By the second act, at least.
BETTY	To please their lordships of the pit, who are so rotten with the pox as to be capable of nothing but looking.
APHRA	Well, we do but fool after all.
HARCOURT	Not altogether fooling, neither. Believe me, madam, I understand the business. Write us just such a piece as this, and I have no doubt —
BETTY	That the sharers will take profits, and we shall — if we have great good fortune — eat. What more may a hireling ask?
HARCOURT	She's out of humour because she's newly out of office. 'Twill not last.

APHRA	How, sir?
BETTY	Do not mind him. He means to be witty in his own person now.
HARCOURT	'Tis the familiar history, madam. After all his promises and vows, her keeper has married an old, rich wife, jealous as the devil, so Mistress Betty must march.
BETTY	Not on foot, sir, that's certain. I've a new horse in view, with a little management, might carry me nobly.
HARCOURT	My lord Greville was in the pit again today. You saw him, I think?
BETTY	I have eyes, sir.
HARCOURT	And they are open. His lordship, you know, has a great mind to see the celebrated authoress.
BETTY	Indeed?
HARCOURT	He has made the attempt on several occasions, but never yet succeeded in his aim. I believe if you should walk in the Park, you would be certain then to meet.
APHRA	Then, sir, I certainly shall not. 'Tis my plays are the spectacle.
HARCOURT	But madam —
APHRA	Sir, your new piece will not write itself. *(counting her "takings")* One comedy's worth. *(separating a sum)* No sooner come than gone. This must to Mr. Godwin tonight. He will not give a day's grace for it. He would have seen me starve in prison rather than lose one farthing of his debt. One day I think I shall throw the money in his teeth, that he may choke upon it for food. *(looking at them and laughing)* Well, perhaps not. You need not look so frightened.

HARCOURT   Godwin's house lies in my way. I will carry your payment to him, if you dare trust me so far.

APHRA   'Twould be a kindness, sir. He's no samaritan. He never sees me but he threatens arrest.

BETTY   And do you keep so little behind?

APHRA   I shall do very well. There is something to come from the bookseller too.

BETTY   Have you sold your comedy, then?

APHRA   *(smiling at HARCOURT)* With a friend's assistance. I have enough now for present need. I can therefore need no more.

HARCOURT   Madam, you are a philosopher too. But now, I fear, I must take my leave. A playhouse will not manage itself neither.

APHRA   Mr. Harcourt. A moment, sir. There is still another favour I would beg.

HARCOURT   You cannot please me better than to make use of me.

APHRA   I have here a piece I have been writing some time. It is not quite — That is, I should be most — If you would look it over, sir?

APHRA gives him the manuscript.

HARCOURT   My dear madam, and is this all? I shall read it with pleasure. Your servant, Mrs. Behn. Till tomorrow, Mrs. Betty. Remember, we begin at *ten* o'clock.

HARCOURT exits.

APHRA   Well?

BETTY   He'll read it, but...I wouldn't expect too much.

APHRA You don't think it's any good.

BETTY Of course it's good.

APHRA He helped me before.

BETTY And he will again. But he can't risk the profits, or we'll all go hungry.

APHRA Would it be such a risk?

BETTY That's not what the public wants. They want fans, and masks, and weddings in the last act.

APHRA Comedy.

BETTY Or if it is tragedy, then on the grand scale. Something splendid, and heroic, and...

APHRA And?

BETTY Impossible. *(as APHRA laughs)* Your heroine isn't even an Indian princess. She doesn't take poison, or go mad, or fall on her lover's sword.

APHRA Every word is true.

BETTY I know. You have to write what they want. You can't afford not to. Give them what they want. Only be sure to make them pay. I always do. Aphra, would you do something for me?

APHRA Of course. Anything I can.

BETTY Go to the Park. And let me come with you.

APHRA No.

BETTY This isn't some country squire, you know. You can't just —

APHRA I know enough about his lordship.

BETTY I don't think you do.

Act One / 165

APHRA	When his uncle dies, he'll be a duke. He dines with Privy Councillors, and he's on his second heiress. I do hear things.
BETTY	I'm going to meet him. At the Park, or...I'm tired of baronets. I think it's time I flew higher.
APHRA	Betty —
BETTY	You won't have to do anything. Just speak a word or two, or curtsey to him even. I'll manage the rest from there.
APHRA	If it's the money, I could —
BETTY	No, you couldn't.
APHRA	You don't have to do this. You're not like the others. You're a great actress.
BETTY	Aren't we all? Aphra, do you think I can live on what they pay me at the theatre? Half of what they give the men and a benefit once a year? If I had a share like Harcourt, it might be different, and he's paid for managing too. What I get now barely keeps me in gloves, and I do so like gloves. It's understood that we'll supplement our income. If you had any sense you'd be doing the same.
APHRA	No.
BETTY	You're mad.
APHRA	Probably.
BETTY	How much is the bookseller giving you?
APHRA	Thirty pounds. It's a fair price. More than fair.
BETTY	Plus the takings from your benefit — not counting your payment, and this quarter's rent.

APHRA As my name gets better known, I'll get more work. And more money for doing it. You'll see.

BETTY And if you don't? You can't write plays in a debtors' prison.

APHRA If I have to, I will.

BETTY I'm not talking about marriage. But if you had a keeper, you could write at leisure. In comfort.

APHRA For as long as it lasted.

BETTY If it were someone with influence, interest. A courtier, say, or —

APHRA Or a lord?

BETTY With someone like that you wouldn't have to care when he left. You'd be established. Aphra, think of it. If you had a keeper, you could write what you wanted.

APHRA If I had a keeper, I couldn't write at all.

BETTY I'll never ask again, I promise. *(no response)* I will do it without you. *(holding out a mask)* Come with me to the Park. Please.

> *APHRA gives in, takes the mask. Music. Both women raise masks to their faces, move to encounter GREVILLE, ARCHER and HOYLE as they walk in the park.*

Three

GREVILLE Madam, I was beginning to fear I had missed you once again. Now you appear, but in clouded glory.

APHRA curtseys, but does not lower her mask.

GREVILLE Still in eclipse? Believe me, you mask in vain. So much wit and genius must discover themselves, conceal them how you will.

APHRA acknowledges the compliment, still does not unmask.

GREVILLE I am but a sorry astronomer. There are some stars, of course, are seen only in season.

BETTY moves forward, lowers her mask.

BETTY Sir, I at least will not hide my light further. Being so far the fainter of the two.

GREVILLE Mistress Lacy. You do yourself an injury, madam. Those who have seen you play once can follow no other planet.

ARCHER Gad, excellently said. "No other planet."

BETTY   I see, my lord, you carry your own chorus with you.

GREVILLE   Being an indifferent performer, I would not take the stage alone.

BETTY   False modesty, sir. You are no amateur. 'Tis well known you've trodden the boards before.

GREVILLE   An interlude or two, I do confess. Brief entertainments, nothing more.

BETTY   Have you no new plot in hand?

GREVILLE   There is a scene I would play out, but it wants private acting.

BETTY   I never play, save to the full applause of the whole house.

GREVILLE   I have no doubt. Do you never give a command performance?

BETTY   That would depend upon the terms of engagement.

GREVILLE   Name them, madam. For I am eager to raise the scene, and would begin the action straight.

BETTY   You must know, sir, a player of my experience—

GREVILLE   Commands a certain fee. That is of course. What more?

BETTY   I act when I like and choose my own time for exits and entrances.

GREVILLE   That must be subject to the approval of the manager.

BETTY   I concede. But no rivals in the wings. The part is my own.

Act One / 169

GREVILLE   The stage would be yours for the length of the run. The season to end at the proprietor's pleasure.

BETTY   Agreed. So fair notice is given to quit.

GREVILLE   Agreed. Shall we retire, madam, and rehearse our parts? I can pledge your satisfaction with the future performance.

BETTY   I know my cue, sir, and require no further prompting.

They exit.

ARCHER   Well said. Gad. Excellently well said. *(addressing APHRA)* Madam, I would beg the favour of a turn or two myself, but, you must know, I am appointed to dine with a certain noble lady.

APHRA   A *noble* lady? Why then, sir, you must not stay indeed. I will bear the disappointment as I may.

APHRA makes a grand gesture of extending her hand to be kissed. ARCHER responds with a flourish. He exits. APHRA addresses HOYLE.

APHRA   Now, sir, you reserved your applause. Were you not pleased with this tender scene?

HOYLE   No, madam. I have seen it acted too many times before. The spectacle is too familiar to impress, and wearies the audience no less than the players.

APHRA   You are for novelty. Are you a critic, sir?

HOYLE   A student, say. I claim no more.

APHRA   You come to watch merely, and are not for a play yourself.

HOYLE   Yet you see we are left to conclude the last act together.

APHRA   The last act so soon? That is unskilful playing.

HOYLE   Too long a prologue will spoil a plot.

APHRA   True. But there's some business needed still before the final curtain.

HOYLE   I yield to your acknowledged skill, and will play the part you write.

APHRA   Comedy or tragedy, sir? You may make your choice.

HOYLE   Neither, I trust. The one must always finish in marriage, the other in death.

APHRA   Might I not write to a different end?

HOYLE   You break forms at your peril, and run the risk of being damned for the attempt.

APHRA   Let it be farce, then. Or perhaps a masque?

HOYLE   No masks with me. I scorn disguise and would have the bare face underneath.

APHRA   Then, sir, you deceive yourself more than disguise could do. *(lowering her mask)* This is the veriest mask of all.

> *Music. APHRA curtseys, moves off to walk. HOYLE looks after her, exits. APHRA continues to walk through the park. BETTY enters, marking a time shift.*

Four

BETTY	I thought you might be here. Mr. Hoyle is not very gallant. He keeps a lady watching in vain.
APHRA	I'm not watching for him.
BETTY	Of course. You take the air for health's sake merely, these — How many weeks past?

APHRA gives in, laughs.

APHRA	Do you know him?
BETTY	Another failed Puritan from what I hear. The Town's still lousy with them. His father was — something in the war. There was a story, I think, or...
APHRA	Or?
BETTY	I can't remember now. But never mind him. I've got some news for you. You know Sir William, don't you?
APHRA	My lord's shadow?
BETTY	That's the one. He tells me he's a great collector of novelties, like lady authors. Naturally, I've promised to do what good offices I can.

APHRA — That chattering spaniel?

BETTY — Aphra, for the sport. Gad, my dear. The sport.

APHRA — 'Tis an excellent night for a fop hunt.

BETTY — Damn me, so 'tis.

ARCHER enters.

BETTY — And here comes your quarry now.

APHRA — *(raising her mask)* Dressed in his most killing airs.

ARCHER advances towards her, bows elaborately. She curtseys with equal formality, deliberately matching him flourish for flourish in an escalation of civility.

ARCHER — Mrs. Behn.

APHRA — Sir William.

ARCHER — *(bowing again)* Madam.

APHRA — *(curtseying in kind)* Sir.

ARCHER — *(another bow)* Your servant.

APHRA — *(a matching curtsey)* Yours. And now, sir, civilities being done, shall we to business? *(ARCHER is taken aback)* Have you some business with me?

ARCHER — Aye, madam, that's the word.

APHRA — To it, sir. To it. So formal a merchant must lose his affairs.

ARCHER — Now that's well said. A good metaphor, indeed.

APHRA	You are too obliging, sir. 'Tis well known you are a connoisseur.
ARCHER	The Town has been pleased to call me so, once or twice.
APHRA	What, no more?
ARCHER	I do not speak it to boast, of course. But I do think —
APHRA	That you have quite forgot your business. And so do I.
ARCHER	Madam?
BETTY	The celebrated Mrs. Behn.
ARCHER	I thank you, madam, for the recollection. *(waving her off)* By your leave. Now, let me see. Oh yes. Mrs. Behn.
APHRA	She is all attention, sir.
ARCHER	Madam. The countless graces of your person, the gentility of your air and charms of your address, the beauty too of your face —
APHRA	My face, Sir William, you do not see. But you know my mask, and that, no doubt, will serve. There is no difference.

HOYLE enters. APHRA notes him.

ARCHER	No difference between a mask and a face? Madam, would you take me for a fool?
APHRA	On the contrary, sir. I would not take you at all. And now, pray excuse me.

APHRA moves off, passing the ball to BETTY who fields it with ease.

ARCHER	Mrs. Behn —

BETTY One turn about the Park, sir, before we leave?

ARCHER But, madam, I had a speech prepared.

BETTY Come, Sir William. You may make your speech to me.

> *Music. BETTY and ARCHER exit as APHRA "accidentally" encounters HOYLE.*

Five

HOYLE	Madam, I had hoped to find you here again.
APHRA	*(unmasking)* And, sir, here I am.
HOYLE	You come for solitude, which I disturb.
APHRA	Solitude, Mr. Hoyle, I seek elsewhere.
HOYLE	Yet you are unattended.
APHRA	I often walk alone. 'Tis one of my pleasures.
HOYLE	A dangerous one, I fear.
APHRA	I have spent whole nights walking alone, before this. In places too that were quite strange to me. You are surprised, perhaps?
HOYLE	It is unusual. But not, I think, so very surprising.
APHRA	The greater the danger, the more precious the liberty. Can you read that riddle, sir?
HOYLE	Madam, I believe I can read it very well.
APHRA	And that too is unusual. But it grows late, sir. I must bid you goodnight.

HOYLE   Mrs. Behn —

APHRA   Mr. Hoyle?

> *They look at each other.*

APHRA   We shall meet again, sir.

> *Music. APHRA exits. HOYLE seats himself, takes up a book, begins reading. Time shift. GREVILLE and ARCHER enter Hoyle's lodgings.*

Six

GREVILLE What, Jack, reading at this hour? I trusted to find you better employed.

HOYLE Can a man be better employed than in study? 'Tis pleasure and profit both.

ARCHER Gad, sir, d'you study for pleasure? That's an odd sort of inclination. I have not taken up a book since I left school. Or, if I have, 'tis very sure I did not read it. This squinting by candlelight, 'tis an occupation for 'prentice boys or clerks. I avoid it entirely myself.

HOYLE Truly, sir, you need not fear. No one will ever mistake you for a scholar.

GREVILLE Now, Diogenes, be civil. We come on a visit of congratulation.

HOYLE Your lordship is too kind. The more as I can call to mind no particular occasion of good fortune.

GREVILLE So uncommon a lady and no occasion? You are ungrateful, sir. There are others would rate your privileges higher.

HOYLE My lord?

GREVILLE   You must not be so modest. You have made a notable conquest, and put poor Sir William, for one, quite out of countenance.

ARCHER   Nay, my lord, I must protest. 'Twould take more than a woman to put me out.

GREVILLE   You speak like a sportsman. One cannot always hit the mark. You shot and missed, frighting the deer into another's sights. And one, I think, who never used to follow that game. Eh, Jack?

ARCHER   For my part, I took the field for sport's sake merely. I have no taste for venison when it has been so long upon the hoof. The meat grows tough, you know, and foully rank. That was neatly turned, I thought.

HOYLE   Neat enough. Though something savouring, perhaps, of disappointment?

ARCHER   "Savouring." That's well turned too. Gad, Mr. Hoyle, you understand a conceit.

HOYLE   Sir.

GREVILLE   We are for Lockett's and a bottle or two. D'you join us, Jack?

ARCHER   We drink at my charge, sir, of course.

HOYLE   Of course. *(indicating his book)* But as you see, I am already engaged.

GREVILLE   A heavy companion for an evening's pleasure. *(examining the book)* But then he's a famous truth-teller too. Come, Sir William, we'll leave the philosopher to his meditations.

ARCHER   My lord.

GREVILLE   Or other nocturnal exercises. Servant, Jack.

HOYLE   My lord. Sir.

GREVILLE and ARCHER exit Hoyle's lodgings. HOYLE returns to his book.

ARCHER   I do not admire the lady's taste.

GREVILLE   Sir?

ARCHER   He's a surly fellow, for all his wit. And not so very handsome neither. Then there's the other business, too.

GREVILLE   I did hear he has not ranged quite so freely of late. The gentleman repents, no doubt, and recovers the light. He comes of a godly line, after all.

APHRA enters, encounters them. GREVILLE bows deeply. She looks him full in the face, curtseys, moves on to Hoyle's lodgings. GREVILLE looks after her.

ARCHER   They're well matched, my lord, would you not say? He has no honour and she no shame.

GREVILLE   Come, Sir William. Lockett's.

They exit. Music. HOYLE registers APHRA's presence.

Seven

APHRA You weren't at the Park last night.

HOYLE You should have worn your mask at least.

APHRA I thought you scorned disguise.

HOYLE For your sake. They're talking already.

APHRA They would be anyhow. Pray, sir, consider your own reputation. Mine you may leave to me.

APHRA holds out her hand for HOYLE's book. He gives it to her.

APHRA De Rerum Natura. On the nature of things. Lucretius.

HOYLE Borrow it, if you like.

APHRA lays the book aside.

HOYLE Why not?

APHRA I don't read Latin.

HOYLE But — I assumed —

APHRA	Wrongly, as it turns out. My brother learned, of course. I used to pick up his grammar and try to decipher it. I read all his books, but the grammar intrigued me. I thought it was a secret language, a code, that only men could learn. Then I grew older and discovered I was right. He did try to teach me once, but my father put a stop to that.
HOYLE	Why?
APHRA	Don't you know the proverb? "A learned woman —"
HOYLE	"— is twice a fool."
APHRA	My father agreed. He thought I would be sufficiently educated if I knew enough to tell my husband's bed from someone else's. Anything more would be superfluous. Wasted. What about your father, did he —

APHRA remembers, stops.

HOYLE	You've heard of him, of course.
APHRA	No.
HOYLE	Sir Thomas Hoyle? The famous regicide? Was there no one to tell you the story? Come, Mrs. Behn, I'll help you. The one who hanged himself. You must have heard that.
APHRA	Yes. I heard.
HOYLE	On the first anniversary of the king's execution he strung himself from a tree at the bottom of our garden. A life for a life. Would you call that poetic justice? Or perhaps you prefer the hand of God. He'd been haunted, by the spectre of a bleeding corpse, without a head. A year to the day he— It is quite true. I can bear witness.
APHRA	You?

HOYLE	Found him, yes.
APHRA	But you couldn't have been more than a child.
HOYLE	I was ten.
APHRA	Dear God. *(with effort)* Do you — Do you read Greek too?
HOYLE	And Hebrew.
APHRA	Naturally. Modern?
HOYLE	French. Italian. Some Spanish.
APHRA	You were lucky. You could translate, you know. There's money in it for someone who's good. But I suppose a Gray's Inn lawyer doesn't worry about things like that.
HOYLE	Is that what you do, translate? The plays alone can't be enough.
APHRA	I've taken a hundred pounds at a single benefit.
HOYLE	But you translate too.
APHRA	Takings can vary. I do French mostly, though I know Dutch as well.
HOYLE	Dutch.
APHRA	I was quite fluent once. I do write other things too.
HOYLE	Poems, and songs. Good ones.
APHRA	They sell.
HOYLE	Is the money so important?
APHRA	You've never been in prison for debt. That's obvious.

HOYLE	It's true, then.
APHRA	Hadn't you heard?
HOYLE	But your husband —
APHRA	Ah yes. My husband.
HOYLE	Didn't he have money?
APHRA	Of course. That was why I married him. Does that shock you?
HOYLE	No.
APHRA	I was going to be secure. Only he died, very suddenly. Without a will. By the time the estate was cleared, there was nothing left for me. I misjudged my advantage. I often do.
HOYLE	Was he old?
APHRA	Yes, rather, but he died of the plague. He was a kind man. Generous. He would have made provision if there'd been time, but...We were only married a year. He sent me to the country when the sickness came. I never saw him after that. It still seems like a dream sometimes. *(looking at him)* Were you here?
HOYLE	Yes.
APHRA	In the city?
HOYLE	Yes.
APHRA	What was it —
HOYLE	Something like being in hell.
APHRA	Would you tell me?
HOYLE	Why?

APHRA I've tried to imagine. Please. I want to know. Please.

HOYLE Empty streets. Houses...deserted, or sealed up, with a red cross on the door and a prayer scrawled underneath. "Lord, have mercy upon us." Mercy. And then at night, the sick and the dying crawling out into the dark to breathe the air. Crowds of living ghosts haunting the city.

APHRA Why didn't you leave?

HOYLE I didn't want to.

APHRA But you might have —

HOYLE I used to walk through the streets at night, looking at the faces. Men and women. Children. Old people.

APHRA Like the Dance of Death.

HOYLE Yes. And I would watch. Does that shock you?

APHRA Were you never afraid?

HOYLE What, of the plague? Of dying?

APHRA Yes.

HOYLE No, not of that.

APHRA What, then?

HOYLE shakes his head, makes some other gesture of warning, dismissal.

APHRA I thought I would die. In the prison. It was — I thought I would be left there until I simply rotted away. And there would be no sign left that I had ever been. No trace. That was the worst of all. That. I even thought of killing myself. To have it over with at once. There were sheets. I could

APHRA	*(continued)* have managed a rope. It wasn't that I was afraid. I refused to die a blank page.
HOYLE	So you wrote.
APHRA	Now I can never be erased. Not entirely. Some faint mark will always remain behind and that will be my sign. My story.
HOYLE	A virtuous woman has no story, they say. She lives and dies unread and unknown.
APHRA	I'm not virtuous. I don't think I ever was.
HOYLE	Neither am I.

They look at each other, break into laughter. HOYLE makes a formal bow.

HOYLE	Your humble servant, madam.

APHRA curtseys, extends her hand.

APHRA	Sir, yours.

HOYLE turns her hand to kiss the palm. Music. Another time shift. HOYLE seats himself, reads. APHRA joins him, writes. She touches him, perhaps rests her hand briefly on his arm, a gesture of intimacy. HOYLE responds. APHRA returns to her work. HOYLE exits quietly. APHRA takes up some papers, reads them, begins to laugh. BETTY enters carrying a bottle of wine and two glasses. Time shift.

Eight

APHRA Did you hear them laughing? Did you? The whole company, even the servants.

BETTY I was there, remember?

APHRA What did they say after I left? What did Harcourt say?

BETTY He thinks it will be brilliant.

APHRA Better than that. *Astraea* has outdone herself this time.

BETTY Who?

APHRA Don't you read any more? *(flourishing the papers)* Three poems to me this week alone. Epics of praise, I can assure you. And some rather lame metre. *(reading)* "To the Ingenious Mrs. Behn."

BETTY "To the Divine Astraea, Sister of the Muse"?

APHRA "Astraea Redux, Or — "

APHRA & BETTY *(together)* "The New Golden Age."

APHRA	And what did she do, after all, good old *Astraea*? The Immortal? The Goddess? The Celestial Virgin? Went around spreading justice, till she gives it up as a bad job and retreats to heaven. She didn't write plays. She didn't make a whole theatre full of people laugh, and cry, and cheer till they were hoarse. I did. I did.

BETTY hands her a glass.

BETTY	I thought you might like to celebrate. I forgot you could get drunk without it. *(toasting)* To a full third day.
APHRA	It's going to run longer than that. Six days, at least. And a revival before the end of the season.
BETTY	Is that what Harcourt thinks?
APHRA	He will.

They drink.

BETTY	Aphra, about poor old Ellis. You were a little...hard on him.
APHRA	Was I? Well, he deserved it. If he adds any more lines to his part, I'll have to put his name on the title page too. I'll swear I'd never heard half that dialogue before.
BETTY	He thinks he's doing you a favour. The lewder he gets, the more they'll applaud.
APHRA	Fop corner, you mean. It's not going down quite so well in the boxes. And I rather draw the line at suffering for other people's smut.

APHRA refills their glasses.

BETTY	Mrs. Behn, I have a new piece to learn.
APHRA	Mistress Lacy, I have a new piece to write.

They drink.

BETTY   Young Russell came by as I was leaving.

APHRA   Did he?

BETTY   Looking very sparkish too. New coat, I'd say.

APHRA   That old one was practically dropping to pieces.

BETTY   I wonder how he managed it. I did hear his creditors had issued a writ.

APHRA   Someone must have lent him something.

BETTY   Yes. That's what I thought.

BETTY looks narrowly at APHRA.

APHRA   It wasn't very much.

BETTY   Aphra...

APHRA   I couldn't let him go to prison.

BETTY   You'll be back there along with him if you keep throwing your money away on every beggarly scribbler who asks.

APHRA   He has real talent. You think so yourself.

BETTY   I think you're hopeless. You waste perfectly good opportunities for securing yourself —

APHRA   That last opportunity was fat, and ugly, and stupid besides.

BETTY   *(overriding her)* — and then you give your money away to some stage-struck boy who'll never pay you back, that's certain.

APHRA   Probably not. Have some more.

APHRA refills.

BETTY Next thing you'll be writing prologues for him too.

APHRA already has.

BETTY Aphra?

APHRA I know. I'm hopeless. And you're...drunk.

APHRA kisses BETTY on the cheek, seats herself to write.

BETTY You're not going to work.

APHRA There's a letter I want to finish. You don't mind, do you?

BETTY Business?

APHRA No.

BETTY Scandal?

APHRA A letter to a gentleman.

BETTY You write to him.

APHRA Yes.

APHRA writes. BETTY watches, remembers, smiles.

BETTY "Sister of the Muse." *(collecting herself to leave)* Good-night, Aphra. It really is a very good play.

BETTY exits. Music. APHRA feels a twinge in her hand, flexes it, continues writing. HOYLE enters, watches her. APHRA registers his presence. Time shift. Note: From this point, APHRA's hands grow increasingly stiff and painful, intermittent spasms at first, then constant arthritis-like pain which will affect other joints as well.

Nine

APHRA I was writing to you. I sent last night too, but you weren't there.

> *HOYLE takes the half-finished letter, reads, looks at her.*

APHRA For a linguist, Mr. Hoyle, you're suspiciously silent. Have I silenced you, Mr. Hoyle?

HOYLE I've never known a woman like you.

APHRA There are no women like me, didn't you know? Because when I write I'm not a woman at all. I'm an author. *Auctor.* That's right, isn't it? The creator of worlds.

HOYLE "In the beginning was the word."

APHRA My words, Jack. Mine. If you only knew the freedom. It's as if...

HOYLE What?

APHRA There are no — limits. For that one moment at least, the prison walls are down.

HOYLE Will you go on writing to me?

APHRA Yes.

They embrace, kiss. HOYLE closes his eyes.

APHRA No. Look at me.

HOYLE does. They embrace. APHRA takes off his coat, impulsively puts it on.

APHRA Do you think I could play a breeches part?

HOYLE Take it off.

APHRA I think I'd make a good boy. My legs aren't bad, and I could swagger, and swear, and —

HOYLE For God's sake, take it off.

APHRA does.

APHRA Jack, what is it? Tell me.

HOYLE kisses her instead. APHRA accepts the embrace, responds. Music. BETTY enters carrying a sheet of manuscript as HOYLE and APHRA separate and he exits. Time shift. BETTY sees HOYLE's coat, picks it up.

Ten

BETTY He's not even rich.

BETTY lays the coat aside.

APHRA Greville's generous, they say.

BETTY It isn't just the money.

APHRA No?

BETTY There are roles I want to play. Get away from all those witty virgins in breeches. He has influence, connections at Court, and with the Wits. With him at my back— At my back. Poor darling, he does get confused sometimes. I want those roles, Aphra. You can understand that, can't you?

APHRA Yes. I understand. *(indicating BETTY's paper)* Verses to you this time?

BETTY No.

APHRA takes the paper, reads.

APHRA
"To Mrs. A.B. On Her Most Recent Appearance Before the Town." Not another sonnet to *Astraea*. *(reading)*

"Poetess Aphra has now changed her luck,
Finds comedies easier won with a — "*(omitting the word)*

"No longer abusing or straining a plot,
Nor fruitlessly taxing a wit she has not,
In bawdy and filth she has gained a great store,
Jack Hoyle pens the rubbish while she plays the whore."

Jack Hoyle.

BETTY
It goes on.

APHRA
So I see. *(reading on)* Now that's a very obvious rhyme for "hunt".

BETTY
It's been circulating at the theatre. You're rather a stranger there these days.

APHRA
It's this translation. And the new play, of course. I hardly see anyone, even Jack. You'd think they'd come up with something new. They've always said I don't write my plays, from the beginning. Except, of course, when the plays don't succeed. Then I'm given full credit.

BETTY
Why don't you reply? Write something? You could.

APHRA
No.

BETTY
Why let them have the last word?

APHRA
Because every time I pick up my pen I incriminate myself more. That's my offense. Not that I write badly, or too freely, but that I write at all.

HARCOURT enters carrying a copy of the verses.

HARCOURT My dear Mrs. Behn. Mistress Betty. I am afraid I interrupt your private conference.

APHRA You are always most welcome, sir.

HARCOURT Perhaps less so when you see my passport.

APHRA takes the paper, reads again.

BETTY We have seen it already. Such things always travel with speed.

HARCOURT I have only a moment, but I —

APHRA crumples the page.

HARCOURT You must not mind it. This will mean a full house, and a notable profit on your next author's day. For all this new cant of morality, there's nothing does a play so much good as to be soundly damned for being bawdy. Tell the Town once 'tis not fit for the hearing, and you'll be turning the sparks away a fourth day running.

APHRA This play they handle so vilely had no other misfortune but that of coming out for a woman's. Had it been owned for a man's, though known to be the lewdest scribbler of the Town, 'twould still have been held a most admirable piece. You know that is true.

HARCOURT If you were to take a man's name ...

APHRA No.

HARCOURT You have said it yourself. What is offensive now would be excellent humour then. You would enjoy full liberty, and there would be no more such attacks.

APHRA No.

HARCOURT	A role, madam, that's all. A part to play, for the nonce.
APHRA	I would stop writing sooner than take up such a mask as that. God, I am sick to death of the subject. Pray, Mr. Harcourt, what news of my play?
HARCOURT	Your last success, madam? Or the next to come?
APHRA	The play you were to read, sir.
HARCOURT	And so I have, Mrs. Behn. But I must study it more closely still.
APHRA	Is it so very difficult a piece?
HARCOURT	Not difficult, and yet...
APHRA	And yet? Not one word more, sir? Not one? You are not usually so slow to speak. "Mrs. Behn, I think we must have a song here." "Madam, the intrigue is not brisk enough. You must lighten it. You must indeed."
HARCOURT	Mrs. Behn —
APHRA	"Believe me, I understand the business." You never lack an opinion, when you choose.
HARCOURT	I give you my solemn word. You shall have an answer, before —
APHRA	I have finished this next?
BETTY	Or the next after that. Playhouse oaths, you know, carry little credit off the stage.
HARCOURT	Mistress Lacy, I never see you but I mourn the day women were first allowed to act. Have a care, madam. Some pretty boy could still take your parts.

BETTY	There is one part at least, sir, he could never play. For want of certain natural gifts.
HARCOURT	And yet might serve the turn. That young Martin, for one. He has the trick, they say.
APHRA	Martin?
HARCOURT	A handsome youth, on my conscience.
BETTY	But scarcely fit for mention here.
HARCOURT	Are you grown so nice now in your conversation?
BETTY	Sir—
APHRA	*(interposing)* But who is he? Some new hireling come from the Nursery?
HARCOURT	Nay, madam. Saving your reverence, Mistress Lacy, nothing more than a common —
BETTY	*(forestalling him)* Sir, you have long outstayed your moment, I think.
HARCOURT	Madam?

BETTY signs for him to leave.

HARCOURT	Why, then, it seems I must take my leave. Mrs. Behn. Mistress Betty.

HARCOURT exits.

APHRA	Have you two been quarrelling again?
BETTY	You don't know, do you?
APHRA	What?
BETTY	That boy. That — Martin.

Act One / 197

APHRA
: What about him? Another molly plying his wares. And good luck to him, if he doesn't get caught.

BETTY
: Hoyle meets him at the playhouse. At least, that's what they say. I was sure you knew.

APHRA
: No.

BETTY
: Lots of them go with boys.

APHRA
: I know that. What else?

BETTY
: Aphra —

APHRA
: There is more, isn't there? There's always more.

BETTY
: Stories, that's all.

APHRA
: Tell me.

BETTY
: Please —

APHRA
: No. Tell me.

BETTY
: During the plague. He used to walk the streets at night, they say, and —

APHRA
: Go on.

BETTY
: And find boys, and —

APHRA stops her with a gesture.

BETTY
: You mustn't blame Harcourt. He didn't know. About Hoyle and— He would never have —

APHRA
: Go away.

BETTY
: Aphra —

APHRA
: Please. Just go away.

BETTY moves to leave.

BETTY   If you love him, I'm sorry.

> *BETTY exits. Music. APHRA is caught by a spasm in her hands. When it has passed she takes up HOYLE's coat, cradles it.*

APHRA   Jack.

> *HOYLE enters.*

Eleven

APHRA What's happened to the boy?

HOYLE Gone.

APHRA Left you?

HOYLE No.

APHRA Is he a prostitute?

HOYLE He wouldn't say so. But he takes money. As much as he can get.

APHRA I heard more, Jack. The part of the story you didn't tell. You used to walk the streets at night. Did you couple there too? In the alleys, like dogs?

HOYLE There were nights they carried bodies past. More of them, and more often, as the sickness spread. I could see them. The plague would brush by us, no farther from me than you are now. It was a city of the dead.

APHRA No. You chose. You could have left. You were free. But you didn't want to. You wanted to stay, and walk the streets, and...Do you go from me to the streets?

HOYLE   No.

APHRA   Just to the playhouse? Where a hundred eyes would be certain to see. If you're caught —

HOYLE   I'll hang. Yes.

APHRA   Jack.

> *APHRA embraces him, kisses him repeatedly. HOYLE responds. The embraces become more passionate.*

APHRA   Not like that. Like the boy.

> *HOYLE recoils.*

APHRA   It's what you want.

HOYLE   No.

APHRA   Then tell me. About the boy, the streets. Did you — Did you fuck him there too? Like the others, before? Is that what you want? Tell me, Jack. Don't turn away. You see, I can read the riddle too. The greater the danger, remember? The more precious the —

HOYLE   Stop it.

APHRA   You could take me there, Jack. Me. In the alley. Against the wall.

HOYLE   Christ.

APHRA   What, is that too far? Are you frightened now? Do I frighten you?

> *APHRA laughs. HOYLE moves to restrain her. She pushes him away.*

APHRA   No.

HOYLE   Aphra —

APHRA   Don't touch me.

They struggle. HOYLE succeeds in quieting APHRA, holding her, kissing her.

APHRA   You should be frightened, Jack.

End of Act One.

Act Two, Scene Twelve

*Music. APHRA is walking in the park.
HARCOURT enters.*

HARCOURT My dear madam — Mrs. Behn —

APHRA Mr. Harcourt. I did not see you, sir. I was dreaming, I think. I am to blame, indeed, for not sending sooner. You come to inquire for the new piece.

HARCOURT No, madam. To beg your pardon.

APHRA My pardon? Impossible. You could not offend me.

HARCOURT And yet I fear —

APHRA You were my benefactor when I had not a friend in the world. The debt I owe you I can never repay. For the other...That was no fault of yours.

HARCOURT If I had known that he— If I had known, I should never have spoken so. Believe me, madam, I would not hurt you.

APHRA I do believe you. And, sir, you could not do it. You have not the will.

HARCOURT He could hurt you.

APHRA	As I could him.
HARCOURT	Then why?
APHRA	The familiar history, perhaps? No, forgive me. You deserve a fairer answer. Only, I have none to give.
HARCOURT	He is a violent man.
APHRA	Not as you think.
HARCOURT	His father, they say —
APHRA	Yes, that much is true. *(clenching her hands)* You can tell me no new stories of him.
HARCOURT	I have given you pain once more.
APHRA	No. I thank you for your care.

GREVILLE and ARCHER enter as HARCOURT kisses APHRA's hand.

APHRA	You must excuse me now. There is a play, sir, that waits.
HARCOURT	And shall I see you at the playhouse?
APHRA	Another day, perhaps.

APHRA exits. HARCOURT looks after her.

GREVILLE	A handsome woman that, Mr. Harcourt.
ARCHER	So she is, Gad. And witty too, no less than handsome. I always say so.
GREVILLE	'Tis her wit, sir, which makes her so. Beauty you may buy at any tavern, and it soon stales. Wit is a commodity less easily achieved.

ARCHER	That's true, my lord. I have found it devilish hard to come by.
GREVILLE	I do not doubt that. What, Mr. Harcourt, lost in thought? You did not used to be so reflective. Do you not agree, sir, give the lady her due, she is a most handsome witty woman?
HARCOURT	As your lordship says.
GREVILLE	And this rare bird falls to Jack Hoyle's preserve, who is too busy starting other game to hunt his own woods as he should. A sad neglect, Sir William, would you not say?
ARCHER	Quite against all the rules of the sport.
HARCOURT	I hope your lordship does not mean to turn poacher? Your own coverts, surely, are excellently stocked.
ARCHER	Aye, but 'tis the nesting season now. And you know, when pheasants brood, a sportsman shifts his prey.
HARCOURT	What? Pheasants brood? Pray speak plainer, sir.
ARCHER	Mistress Betty. Fie, Mr. Harcourt, how slow you are. You do not keep up to the mark at all.
HARCOURT	With child, by his lordship?
GREVILLE	She tells me so. And I know no reason to doubt her word.
HARCOURT	I pity her.
GREVILLE	You waste your tenderness, sir. She knows her remedy, if she would choose.
HARCOURT	Once she is seen to be with child, she will not be let upon the stage. The ladies of quality will cry scandal, and I must give her parts away.

GREVILLE	They always hate a whore who has been found out, and would have her sin in secret. As honourable ladies do.
ARCHER	Damned hypocrites. Gad, so they are all. Women are all hypocrites by nature.
GREVILLE	Actresses, Sir William, more accomplished than any the playhouse can boast.
HARCOURT	She will suffer for this, my lord.
GREVILLE	Well, sir, I shall maintain her till she has whelped. I never turn off a servant without warning.
ARCHER	A most generous resolution. For you know, Mr. Harcourt, if women will be breeding —
GREVILLE	Yes, Sir William, as you say. But they wait for you at Will's, do they not?
ARCHER	My lord?
GREVILLE	I would not deprive the company of its chief ornament. I shall join you there, by and by.
ARCHER	They do stay my coming, I believe. *(taking his leave)* My lord.
GREVILLE	Sir.

ARCHER exits.

GREVILLE	And now, Mr. Harcourt, I would have a word or two.
HARCOURT	As your lordship pleases.
GREVILLE	Of Mrs. Behn.
HARCOURT	I did not think that was a subject of interest still.

GREVILLE	You think me as shallow as Sir William then, who cares only for following the latest wonder. Her last piece has given offense, I hear.
HARCOURT	There was some objection, my lord.
GREVILLE	A little too free for my lady Prudish and her sister critics? They are in full cry against her now.
HARCOURT	These things go by fashion, and fashions change.
GREVILLE	They envy her liberty, for all their scandal, and rattle their own chains the harder to drown her out. And yet it strikes me, too, a woman who writes so warmly of love, cannot be cold on the subject herself. You did not hear me, Mr. Harcourt? Such a woman, I said, cannot be cold.
HARCOURT	Nor is not, my lord, as I believe.
GREVILLE	Believe, Mr. Harcourt, then you do not know?
HARCOURT	I, sir? How should I know?
GREVILLE	The Town has said —
HARCOURT	The Town, my lord, does me too much honour. And so do you.
GREVILLE	Have you never acted a scene together then? Bought her favours with the promise of a six days' run?
HARCOURT	Never, my lord, and do not think she may be had at such a rate.
GREVILLE	A woman of honour perhaps?
HARCOURT	Truly, sir, as she understands the word.

GREVILLE   She may understand what she will by it. To be esteemed, as the world goes, a woman must be unknown, not catalogued on bills and posted for all to read.

HARCOURT   Her name, it is true, is subject to public handling. Her honour, I think, remains her own.

GREVILLE   Stoutly maintained. Hoyle has her then for nothing, d'you say?

HARCOURT   I do believe so, if love be nothing.

GREVILLE   You may spare your playhouse jargon, sir. Do not mistake me for some City matron in a box.

HARCOURT   My lord.

GREVILLE   Is the gentleman so favoured? Is he so? Yet I'm certain she's neither blind nor a fool. He's taken to wandering again, I hear. So secure in possession, you see, he leaves the field and fears no rivals. That's like his insolence too. Lawyer Jack. Scholar Jack. Plain, honest Jack, whose single grace lies in he will not lie. He's no hypocrite, not he. An upstart ironmonger's son who takes upon himself to judge his betters and flaunts his honesty to all the world. A precious saint, who buggers gutter-ware in the street. He's a true heir of the Commonwealth. They did always love the Rump. But she, to know all, see all, and still to — *(breaking off)*

HARCOURT   To what, my lord?

APHRA enters her lodgings carrying a purse, seats herself.

GREVILLE   Now, if she were put to the proof? The lady might thank me for the attention. And I would leave her no worse for it. *(moving to exit)* Come, Mr. Harcourt. You at least, I think, have no cause to wish Jack Hoyle well.

HARCOURT　　I am at your disposal, my lord. As ever.

They exit. Music. Time shift. APHRA spills coins from the purse. She counts them with difficulty, painfully returning them one by one. HOYLE enters, watches, takes the purse from her, collects and returns the coins, hands the purse back. APHRA empties it and begins again.

Thirteen

HOYLE I heard it was a small house.

APHRA The King's Company had a new play on. That always eats into an author's day. I've made my payment though. And I've started on a new piece. A farce. Surely, even the moralists can't object to Harlequin. Two weeks this time. Why?

HOYLE You were writing. You didn't need me.

APHRA I always need you.

HOYLE Not when you're writing. I wanted you last night.

APHRA I was walking.

HOYLE Where? *(no answer)* In the Park? At the Exchange? The Piazza? Where?

APHRA I want to see the streets, Jack. You have gone back there, haven't you?

HOYLE Is that what his lordship told you? He visits here now, they say.

APHRA I want to see. Where you —

HOYLE No.

APHRA	I've imagined —
HOYLE	No.
APHRA	A hundred times.
HOYLE	Blind alleys. Overflowing gutters. No light. No air.
APHRA	More.
HOYLE	Don't test me. Don't —
APHRA	Intrude? Why? Is there only room in hell for you?
HOYLE	You're mad.
APHRA	When I walk now, Jack, I look for you. And I remember. "Empty streets. Houses deserted or sealed up." I see the crosses on the doors, bodies carried by me.
HOYLE	No.
APHRA	I'll follow you, I swear.
HOYLE	Be quiet, can't you?
APHRA	How will you stop me?
HOYLE	I said —
APHRA	You can't stop me.

HOYLE grabs at her, forgetting her hands. APHRA cries out. He releases her in alarm.

APHRA	I won't be silent, Jack. Not with you.
HOYLE	Aphra —

HOYLE nurses her hands, kisses them.

APHRA   Are you afraid I won't be sufficiently revolted?

HOYLE freezes.

APHRA   Is that what frightens you, after all? *(silence)* Jack, what if I promised to hate you for it?

HOYLE takes up APHRA's mask, holds it out to her. She takes it, lays it aside. HOYLE continues into the street, APHRA following. Music. They walk.

Fourteen

HOYLE: They used to light fires, to burn off the pestilence. Fires at every corner. The smoke would hang over the streets like the disease itself. You could smell it. Taste it. Is this what you want to see?

APHRA: Show me where. Show me.

They walk on. HOYLE stops.

APHRA: Here?

HOYLE is silent. APHRA looks around her.

APHRA: Is it always the same place?

HOYLE: In Christ's name, what sort of woman are you?

APHRA: I saw things, Jack. In the prison. Do you think you're the only one —

HOYLE: There is infection here. Don't you understand?

APHRA: I want to know. I want to feel what you feel.

HOYLE: You can't.

APHRA: If you're tainted, so am I.

HOYLE   No.

APHRA   I whored myself for a whole year. For security. A home.

HOYLE   You had no choice.

APHRA   I could have starved first. God will forgive us. He'll forgive us both.

HOYLE   "Lord have mercy upon us." Should I write that on my plague door too?

APHRA   Jack —

HOYLE   "If I sin, then Thou markest me and Thou wilt not acquit me of mine iniquity." I was taught to say that before I could understand the words. Every night, before I went to bed. "If I sin then Thou markest me." What sort of mercy should I pray for now? Can you tell me that?

APHRA   No.

HOYLE   My father read the Bible aloud on Sundays. Whole chapters at a time. I remember, "Suffer the little children to come unto me and forbid them not, for of such is the kingdom of Heaven." It was a Sunday that he killed himself. I went out into the garden — I can't remember why — and there was something hanging among the trees. At first I couldn't recognize his face. I was only ten. "Suffer the little children to come unto me." I was frightened. I called to him. Reached out. I wanted to—

APHRA   What? Jack, please.

HOYLE   Last night. There was a boy, here, a child, and I... "Father, I have sinned against Heaven and in Thy sight."

APHRA   No.

Act Two / 215

HOYLE God —

APHRA Listen to me.

HOYLE — help me.

APHRA There is grace in love, Jack. And forgiveness. I know. There will be mercy. There must. Look at me, Jack. I love you. Now, God help me. What does that make me? What sort of woman?

APHRA moves to him. He moves away. HARCOURT enters with BETTY. She is masked and leans heavily on him.

HARCOURT Mrs. Behn? Aphra?

APHRA *(seeing BETTY)* No.

HARCOURT She would come out. I could not let her venture alone.

BETTY slumps against him. HOYLE moves to help support her.

APHRA My lodgings. Quickly.

They move to Aphra's lodgings. HOYLE and HARCOURT lead BETTY to a chair. HARCOURT moves to exit. HOYLE bows to him. HARCOURT returns the bow.

HARCOURT Sir.

HARCOURT exits. APHRA and HOYLE look at each other. HOYLE exits.

Fifteen

BETTY Will you take this thing off? I can't breathe.

> *APHRA unties BETTY's mask, lays it aside.*

BETTY That's better. I suddenly felt it was smothering me.

APHRA You shouldn't have come out yet. It's too soon.

BETTY I had to. I couldn't bear those rooms another day. I hear there's a rumour in Town that I helped nature a little. So I could get back to work. It isn't true.

APHRA I know that.

BETTY Not that I haven't before. I wanted a daughter, can you imagine? A son he would have taken from me, but not a little girl. He would have had no use for her and she would have been my own.

APHRA All your own.

BETTY I still bleed for her. From inside. The doctor says it's normal, but Aphra, I don't think I'll ever stop bleeding.

APHRA Yes, you will. You will.

Act Two / 217

APHRA holds her. BETTY clings a moment.

APHRA You must let me help you now.

BETTY You do help me.

APHRA I mean with money.

BETTY No.

APHRA Please.

BETTY I don't need it. Truly, I don't.

APHRA How will you manage?

BETTY The theatre is bringing out a new play. A tragedy. Harcourt's given me a very good part. And it's not just pity either. The Town will flock to see me again. The scandal sheets and lampoons have guaranteed that. Have you seen the latest?

APHRA Yes.

BETTY They hate us both very much, don't they? I think I'll play this new part rather well. I murder the seducer who abandoned me and then stab myself. I have a long final scene of remorse and madness all my own. I imagine I see my lover's ghost, and plead with him to return the innocence he stole. In verse, of course. Lots of poetic frenzy and collapsing in heaps. Then, when I'm tired of that, I kill myself with the dagger I had buried in his heart and die with the words "Now justice is done". Women always die in men's plots, have you noticed? Still, it is a good part. It may well be my best performance yet. Tragedy. Harcourt thinks I have a feeling for the form.

APHRA Lord Greville has been coming here. Did you know?

BETTY   I heard.

APHRA   I go out when I can, but I have to work and he is very...persistent.

BETTY   Yes.

APHRA   I suppose, now you're almost well, he'll leave me in peace.

BETTY   I doubt it.

APHRA looks at her.

BETTY   I've been paid off. After my— mishap. He came to see me, once. Congratulated me on the unexpected conclusion of my business and offered me money, which I took. Rather a large sum. He was always generous. Most wouldn't even give money.

APHRA   He's finished with you, so he comes to me.

BETTY   What difference does it make?

APHRA   Don't you see? It's a more exquisite insult this way.

BETTY   It doesn't matter.

APHRA   Yes, it does. *(taking up pen and paper)* Are you in a creative humour, Betty? I've just had an idea for a poem.

BETTY   No.

APHRA   *(writing)* "To My Lord G."

BETTY   For God's sake, have you forgotten what happened to Freeman? For two lines in a prologue. For a joke.

Act Two / 219

APHRA	Would his lordship send someone to break my arms, do you think? Slit my nose? Crop my ears?
BETTY	You can't afford to offend him. Not now.
APHRA	You let him do this, without a word, a sound. You're as guilty as he is.
BETTY	I never said I wasn't.
APHRA	And I'm guilty too.
BETTY	Listen to me. If you refuse to see him, you'll only hurt yourself. And you won't help me. He doesn't forgive an injury. Aphra, you can't do anything. You can't—
APHRA	Say anything. No. *(taking up BETTY's mask) Femme coverte.* Do you know what that means?
BETTY	No.
APHRA	I'd never heard of it either. My husband explained it to me. It's a law term. Literally it means "covered woman".
BETTY	I don't understand.
APHRA	When a woman marries, she becomes a *femme coverte.* Her legal existence is made inseparable from her husband's. Not just her property, her very existence. She is covered. I've always remembered that. The covered woman. The masked woman. Betty, I think, if I were to write my tragedy now, I think it would be silent. No words at all. And that silence would hold all the voices that never speak, of all the women who are never heard. Covered women, who live and die and leave no history behind except a few lines on a tombstone. Wife of. Sister to. Daughter. Widow. Four possibilities, no more. And even in death our stories are written by someone else.

BETTY	No. Not yours.
	HARCOURT enters carrying manuscript.
HARCOURT	Mrs. Behn. Mistress Betty. I am glad to see you both.
BETTY	Sir.
APHRA	Your servant.
HARCOURT	Your hands are better today, I trust?
APHRA	Thank you, sir. I do not complain.
HARCOURT	Faith, madam, you never do. I met his lordship in the Park. He intends a visit shortly, I believe.
BETTY	Do you come to give warning? Or to prepare his way?
HARCOURT	I come on business, madam.
BETTY	And so does his lordship. Unless I mistake.
HARCOURT	Mrs. Behn, I have told him you are not quite well. He will not be persuaded. He pretends I seek only to put him off, and use the occasion to plead some other patron's suit.
BETTY	And do you?
HARCOURT	No, Mistress Lacy, I do not. Whatever you might think.
APHRA	Come, sir, you had business, you said. You may speak freely. We are all friends.
HARCOURT	I hope you know I am your friend?
APHRA	You have often given proof of that.

Act Two / 221

BETTY   To us both, Mr. Harcourt. And we thank you for it.

HARCOURT   I would do more yet. Nay, I will. But madam — Mrs. Behn —

                    HARCOURT fumbles with the manuscript.

APHRA   I understand you, sir. You need say no more.

HARCOURT   Mrs. Behn, you must let me speak.

APHRA   Why, sir, I understood your long silence well. It is a language I am skilled in.

HARCOURT   Madam?

APHRA   You must return this to me. Come. Why should you be burdened with such useless lumber?

HARCOURT   No burden, madam. Nor no lumber neither. A work of credit, and yet so very...bitter a piece.

BETTY   As life is, sir, some might say.

HARCOURT   Your heroine misused, betrayed, attacked on every side. Left alone at the last, neither widow, maid, nor wife. And yet she lives on, past the final act. The Town will not countenance such a moral. It violates all rules of form.

APHRA   Life again, sir, brings the same complaint. It rarely observes the decorums of art.

HARCOURT   And need I tell you, and now, they do not come to the playhouse to see life? If you would —

APHRA   Alter it?

HARCOURT   No, not entirely. Soften merely. The design something less singular, perhaps, and the wit less —

APHRA	Fierce.
HARCOURT	You might do it easily.
APHRA	So I might. A trifling alteration, as you say. Punish the lady and reward her persecutors. That would suit for a moral. Or, if it will not, I must simply kill her. One way or t'other, she must not escape.
HARCOURT	Mrs. Behn —
BETTY	Aphra, you would not lose it all.
APHRA	Yes, I would. She would be merely a heroine then. I thank you for your good counsel, sir. *(to BETTY)* And yours. But I fear the lady must take her chance.
HARCOURT	I am sorry, madam. It is not in my power.

GREVILLE enters unnoticed, listens.

APHRA	Nor mine, to speak when I may not be heard.
BETTY	The other house, if you were to —
APHRA	I have already, and they say the same. Another piece they would take with pleasure, but not this. Truly, I expected no more. We understand the business, do we not?
BETTY	What will you do with your tragedy now?
APHRA	Burn it, perhaps.
HARCOURT	Mrs. Behn —
BETTY	No.
APHRA	'Twould make a fitting end. They do burn still, for witchcraft, and petty treason, and such like feminine offenses. Only think what a splendid blaze.

GREVILLE   By all means, madam, set it alight. You might then warm yourself at the flame at least. Pray, pardon my intruding again so soon, Mrs. Behn. Mistress Lacy, your servant, ma'am. Your late indisposition quite passed off, I trust? Mr. Harcourt, are you here too? Now, sir, this is unkind. Though you warn me away, you do not scruple to visit yourself, and would deny me a pleasure you still enjoy.

HARCOURT   I come on business, my lord, and can only regret the trouble I bring. Which I do, most heartily.

GREVILLE   Why, then, to make amends, you must take it away again. Do not, Mr. Harcourt, linger on my account. I would not put you to an inconvenience. You have some playhouse affairs to attend to, no doubt. And Mrs. Betty too. Do you not?

APHRA shakes her head at HARCOURT.

GREVILLE   Do you not?

HARCOURT   My lord.

HARCOURT and BETTY move to exit. GREVILLE takes up BETTY's mask.

GREVILLE   Mistress Lacy. You have forgot this, I think.

BETTY takes the mask. They exit.

GREVILLE   So, *exeunt omnes*.

APHRA   So much Latin I understand. They all go out.

GREVILLE   And a new scene may now begin. The stage must always be cleared before. But there is one player wanting still. Where is Jack?

APHRA   I have not seen him this week at least.

GREVILLE   You surprise me, I vow.

APHRA   Do I, my lord?

GREVILLE   Madam, in this as in all things.

APHRA   I have had much writing. And Mr. Hoyle too has business elsewhere.

GREVILLE   His old business, perhaps? *(looking at her)* So it is true. Now, what a careless fellow he is. He seems positively to court detection. But that's the worst of your honest dealers. They never know when to leave off. It has occurred to me, of late, that a word or two spoken in the right ear would hang our honest friend for certain. And there would be an end of all his railing. Do you not agree, Mrs. Behn? I believe you once understood such things.

APHRA   He is, my lord, so careless of himself, he need fear nothing anyone else can do. Even his friends.

GREVILLE   Justly said. Your wit never fails you. Tell me, madam, are your affections as untiring? I think they must be. And yet they buy you nothing but neglect. *(no response)* We are alike, you know, you and I.

APHRA   In nothing, my lord.

GREVILLE   We neither of us deal in half measures. You get no money from him, I'm told.

APHRA   I ask for none.

GREVILLE   The poverty is the same, however it is achieved. I know your story, better than you think. It has been my study for some time.

APHRA   Are you certain, my lord, you know all?

Act Two / 225

GREVILLE — I know you can never save one who is resolved to drown. Can you say you know as much? *(no response)* Old debts still press you, and you are sometimes ill. Your last pieces too have scarce pleased since your farce. And you have long since ceased to be the novelty you once were. It does run so, Mrs. Behn, does it not?

APHRA — You state the case fairly. I am something pressed. I live as I write, from day to day, and cannot see beyond.

GREVILLE — The remedy is near at hand. Why should genius want, when it may be so easily supplied?

APHRA — Do you turn patron now, my lord?

GREVILLE — Might I not take the part? I am not without interest and means. Such means, I fear, as must always be quite beyond your power. I would do you that good I can.

APHRA — And in return?

GREVILLE — Some kindness to me, I would expect. To me alone, you understand.

APHRA — A double revenge, with a single act. That is well plotted.

GREVILLE — Madam?

APHRA — You do not forgive an injury, my lord. And honesty is the greatest of injuries.

GREVILLE — Mrs. Behn, pray reserve your heroics. We are not playing at tragedy now. Will you lose your advantage for the sake of Jack Hoyle? An atheist and sodomite professed. An offender against all authorities and believer in none. His father was a most notorious rebel. A canting Puritan. Nay, a regicide, who would doubtless have died had he not forestalled the hangman by his own act. And

GREVILLE *(continued)* Jack continues the family trade. Faith is wasted on such a man.

APHRA The faith is to myself, not to him. And that is not for hire. I will keep silence for ever rather than once be heard on the terms you offer.

GREVILLE Brave words, indeed. Fit for our friend Mrs. Betty to rant. Yet think what you sacrifice, and for whom.

APHRA Believe me, sir, I do.

GREVILLE lays a purse on the table.

GREVILLE A voluntary tribute. So I may show myself generous too.

GREVILLE moves to exit.

APHRA My lord. *(holding out the purse)* You have forgot this, I think.

GREVILLE takes it from her.

GREVILLE The coin was current, madam. 'Twould have served your need.

Music. HOYLE enters to see GREVILLE kiss Aphra's hand. He moves to leave, encounters HOYLE, bows to him, exits. HOYLE watches as APHRA slowly and painfully begins to write.

Sixteen

HOYLE You need a physician.

HOYLE attempts to take APHRA's hands. She draws them away.

APHRA I've seen one. He prescribed rest.

HOYLE What does my lord Greville prescribe?

APHRA The Town has me dying of the pox, I hear. The perfect moral to my shameless story. How disappointed they'll be when they find out the truth. If they ever do.

HOYLE Why does he come here still? What does he want?

APHRA What do you think? I think you're going to be informed against, Jack. Do you care?

HOYLE His lordship, of course.

APHRA I thought you'd be pleased.

HOYLE And you sent for me to warn me. Your grateful servant, Mrs. Behn. But there is something more, I think. Pray, command me, madam. So signal a favour deserves a return.

APHRA	Stop it. I want — I need you to give me back my letters.
HOYLE	What?
APHRA	There's a bookseller who's willing to bring them out as a volume. A tale of love in letters. I'll change the names, of course. Something classical, I think, in Latin. And I won't use them all. I need the money.
HOYLE	Is there anything you won't sell? You sold yourself to a husband first of all. Then to the government for a spy. Was he your lover too, the man you went to Antwerp to betray? They say he was.
APHRA	They say. You've been listening to stories, Jack.
HOYLE	How much will Greville offer you? Is selling me included in the price?
APHRA	Be careful of him, for God's sake.
HOYLE	Answer me. Tell me.
APHRA	What? That I've betrayed you? Is that how the story is supposed to end? I'm sorry to disappoint you, Jack. It seems there is one thing, after all, I wouldn't do for you. You'll never forgive me, will you, for loving you? That was always the one unpardonable sin.

HOYLE moves to exit.

APHRA	My letters, Jack. Those words are mine.
HOYLE	Then take them.

HOYLE sweeps papers off the table, exits. Music. APHRA collects and sorts her letters. She reads snatches, visibly affected. She clears her table, exits carrying all papers and writing paraphernalia. BETTY enters, seats herself at the bare table. APHRA enters, joins her. Time shift.

Seventeen

APHRA   I'm dying, aren't I?

BETTY   They say so.

APHRA   Then it must be true.

They laugh.

APHRA   I'm glad.

BETTY   Aphra —

APHRA   Look at my hands. They're ugly. And they hurt.

BETTY   I know.

APHRA   No. I never imagined anything could hurt so much. I finished my pages, though. They went to the bookseller yesterday. Harcourt took them.

BETTY   He's going to revive your farce again. New scenes, new costumes too. Did he tell you?

APHRA   Yes. Funny to think that should prove my most successful piece. All my hopes of fame to rest on a farce. Betty, will you do something for me?

BETTY   Yes.

APHRA	Will you see Jack, afterwards? Will you tell him I commissioned him to write my epitaph? I trusted the last word to him. Will you?
BETTY	Yes. *(pause)* Aphra. Your play, your tragedy...
APHRA	You almost missed the bonfire.

BETTY looks at her, hurries out. APHRA waits. BETTY reenters.

BETTY	Ashes.
APHRA	Yes.
BETTY	Why? Why would you —
APHRA	It wasn't what I remembered. I thought I knew so much then. After the prison and...I thought there was nothing more to know.
BETTY	It was a good play.
APHRA	And I was free to destroy it. No one could stop me doing that. My choice. You see, don't you? You understand?
BETTY	Yes. I understand.
APHRA	They used to light fires, during the plague. In the streets. Fires at every corner. Did you know?
BETTY	No.
APHRA	You will see him? You'll tell him?
BETTY	Yes.
APHRA	Promise me.
BETTY	I do promise.

APHRA reaches out her hand. BETTY takes it. APHRA starts with the pain. BETTY releases her hand.

APHRA No. Don't let go.

BETTY takes her hand again, holds it.

APHRA Will you stay until the fire burns out?

BETTY Yes.

Music. APHRA and BETTY exit. HOYLE, GREVILLE, HARCOURT and ARCHER enter a tavern. They drink. Time shift.

Act Two / 233

Eighteen

GREVILLE So the divine *Astraea* has taken her flight to heaven. She has played her scene and brought the curtain down, for the last. I knew how it must end.

ARCHER They do say she died in great poverty, my lord.

HARCOURT But free of debt. She had paid all.

ARCHER As to that, Mr. Harcourt, I heard she was kept by you these last months.

GREVILLE That was most generous of you. For I am sure you can have but little to spare.

ARCHER And she in no condition to repay.

HARCOURT I would have spared all I could, my lord, and gladly. But she would take nothing. She kept herself, until the end.

GREVILLE Well, she had courage. And I will drink to that. *(toasting)* Mrs. Behn.

ARCHER Mrs. Behn.

GREVILLE You do not join us, Mr. Harcourt?

HARCOURT Mrs. Behn.

GREVILLE   A very pretty, witty whore. But like all whores she never knew her proper price.

ARCHER   An epitaph, my lord. You have hit it, exact.

GREVILLE   I once thought to venture in her market, having no better diversion to hand, and made an offer fairly. But she was coy and would stand out for more. A mercenary slut, like the rest of her sex.

HOYLE   You lying bastard. God damn you for a liar.

HOYLE throws the contents of his glass in GREVILLE's face. They rush at each other, scrambling and fighting viciously. HARCOURT separates them with difficulty.

HARCOURT   He is drunk, my lord. In Heaven's name, he is drunk.

GREVILLE   Why so he is, Mr. Harcourt. But have a care, Jack. You will go too far one day.

HOYLE bows. GREVILLE exits.

ARCHER   Gad, Mr. Hoyle. What fool's trick is this?

HOYLE makes a feint as if to spring. ARCHER recoils. HOYLE laughs. ARCHER turns to HARCOURT.

ARCHER   Were I his lordship, I would run him through. He is too mean a fellow to fight with.

ARCHER exits. HARCOURT retrieves HOYLE's glass, generally restores order.

HARCOURT   It does her no good now.

HARCOURT exits. Music. APHRA enters, carrying a mask.

Epilogue

HOYLE Aphra.

APHRA Was that for me? Did you do that for me? It doesn't matter what they say. They never got the story straight. A fight with a stranger in the street. At night. That's how it will end. You know that, don't you?

HOYLE Yes. In the street.

APHRA Will you be frightened?

HOYLE No.

APHRA Jack, tell me. Were there always shadows? Ghosts? Even at the beginning, when we first —

HOYLE No, not always. You were...Not always.

APHRA smiles.

APHRA Thank you for the epitaph.

HOYLE It should have been Poets' Corner.

A Woman's Comedy / 236

APHRA I never thought they'd let me get this close. Eastern cloister. There's an obscure Victorian clergyman who's going to be outraged. "The late ingenious Mrs. Behn. Author of diverse plays, poems and other works. Died the sixteenth day of April in the year sixteen hundred and eighty-nine. Here lies a proof that wit can never be/Defence enough against mortality." You were never very good with verse. I could rewrite it. "Aphra Behn. *Auctor.*"

HOYLE It isn't very much, for a life.

APHRA Creator of worlds. It's enough.

Music. HOYLE exits. APHRA lays her mask aside, looks out.